Grey Friars

This book is dedicated to all who have
contributed to the Grey Friars experience.

Grey Friars

Opening the Door to Adult Education

Dorothy Schwarz, Maggie Freeman, Alan Skinner

Access Books
COLCHESTER

The imprint of CALCAG
Colchester Adult Learning Continuing Access Group - Charity 1095713

Access Books
Willow Cottage, Staffords Corner, Great Wigborough,
Colchester, CO5 7RP

First published in Great Britain by Access Books, 2005

ISBN-10: 0-9551826-0-3
ISBN-13: 978-0-9551826-0-0

British Library Cataloguing-in-Publication Data
A CIP catalogue record is available for this book from the British Library.

Colour photography:

Outer cover:
Stephanie Mackrill Photography
Colchester 514416
www.stephaniemackrill.com

Inner cover and centre colour section:
Harland Payne Photo
Colchester 768592
www.harlandpaynephoto.com

Printed in Great Britain by
Palladian Press
Colchester
Essex

Contents

Foreword

Baroness Helena Kennedy QC

Grey Friars is a special place. It should be on the Grand Tour of every new education minister before wheels are reinvented and new-fangled schemes are cobbled together to deal with skills shortages and social exclusion, anti-social behaviour and civic regeneration.

The reason Grey Friars is special is because it is in the business of changing people's lives, reaching parts that are otherwise not reached, substituting positive experiences of learning for the negative, sometimes compensating for what went wrong first time round, at other times adding to the curiosity and hunger to learn of an already lively mind. It keeps on doing what the best adult educational establishments have always done but it does it with a unique verve, passion and commitment.

Grey Friars' story needs to be told. Here is a college which was widening participation before the words became the contemporary mantra. It has always reached out to the disadvantaged, providing access to Higher Education before access courses were invented, removing barriers, inventing routes into new worlds, providing nurseries for babies as well as toddlers so that young mothers can have an education. Innovation has always started there. Grey Friars was measuring for high quality standards of teaching before 'professional competence' became a byword. It has always built progression into its courses and has always worked collaboratively with other institutions.

However, what is at the heart of Grey Friars' success is the ethos shared by all the staff that there is no hierarchy of worth, no learner more important than any other, no subject more important than any other, no motivation or level of learning more valued than any other. All learning is fostered because it is recognised that when people have lost confidence or breathed in failure because of negative early experiences of schooling, the first steps back may be small. However, those first small steps may be the beginning of an incredible journey.

I always claim that criminal lawyers have the best stories. If you are going to be stuck on a slow train, it is better not to be stuck with an insurance salesman. Criminal lawyers usually have a raft of yarns about the miscreants they have represented and the hours always sail by. However after I took evidence for my report Learning Works, I decided that teachers in Adult Education have the most life-enhancing stories because this is where extraordinary transformation takes place. It also became clear to me that opportunities to learn are at the heart of real regeneration projects. Here is the way to strengthen communities, support families, create active citizens, keep old people active, encourage independence in the young and help people of all ages discover new ways of seeing.

Adult Education is always described as the Cinderella of the education system: neglected, unsung and poorly resourced, yet glorious, magical and just waiting to be recognised for all its brilliance. The arguments are so plain; the evidence so clear; the extraordinary life changing stories there to be told. If only government could see the extraordinary riches that come from this amazing part of our civic society, the Treasury would dig into its coffers and pour its bounty into this secret garden.

This book makes the argument better than any of us can. Grey Friars is the exemplar. It should be celebrated, strengthened and emulated around the country.

Introduction

Alan Skinner MBE

For a hundred years Grey Friars has been a place of education, first as a school and for the last thirty years as an adult college. Tens of thousands of local people have passed through its doors. Its influence and capacity to change lives has been immense. It comes as no surprise therefore to learn that Grey Friars occupies a special place in the affections of the community it serves.

Education touches everyone's life. Experiences of education can range from a positive beginning, with the individual going from strength to strength as he or she successfully progresses through the system, to negative early encounters from which it is an almost impossible struggle to recover. In the case of people in this latter group, who may have been affected by health, social pressures or low expectations, education is as vital in their own lives as it is in the lives of their children.

Adults have demanding, complicated lives, which can be affected by major changes due to family or employment problems, and the first responsibility of a good adult education service is to recognise this fact, to be responsive to their needs. The extraordinary diversity of the needs and attitudes of adult learners means that the timing, form and structure of the learning experience must be supremely flexible.

Adult learners, especially the vulnerable and disadvantaged, need a reliable education service they can trust which provides continuity and flexibility and is demonstrably open to all.

Nothing has been as effective and enduring as the existence of an identifiable and reliable local adult education centre, collaborating and co-operating from a significant base that is accepted as a welcoming, stimulating, inclusive and relevant adult environment.

Adults also need a comprehensive curriculum, which can be modified according to changing national and local priorities, rather than a confusing and narrow collection of ephemeral 'opportunities'. People have no affinity with such paternalistic arrangements, but, nevertheless, they pay for them through taxation.

Successive governments have made education a major part of their plans for the country's development. But education policies need time for their effectiveness to be properly evaluated – and this has not always been allowed.

Also, further, adult and higher education have to compete with the schools sector, and each other, for attention and funding. The education of adults, almost always the poor relation, has occasionally achieved a higher profile, as in the Russell Report under Mrs Thatcher, or, more recently, when David Blunkett was Minister for Education and he accurately extolled the benefits of lifelong learning. However, adult education is too easily relegated when the focus switches to the needs of younger people, be they in the school or post-school sectors.

The education of adults is far too important to individuals, families, communities and the nation to be funded by here-today-gone-tomorrow schemes, operated by here-today-gone-tomorrow quangos. What it desperately needs is a period of stability in order to develop effectively over at least a ten-year period so that people may clearly map their way through a coherent and reliable set of opportunities.

Local people deserve a strategically-planned and sustainable adult education system if they are to take part in – and help to sustain – a culture of lifelong learning both nationally and in their communities.

This book is about such people – the rich diversity of those who come to learn. It is also about the passion and commitment of tutors, support staff, managers and administrators who come together to form a community of learners.

The energy generated from their motivations, aspirations and interaction provides a creative spark - that special ingredient which separates a good adult learning experience from a routine training exercise. Adult education inspires and enables people to become not just consumers, but participants with a sense of belonging and security.

Whether in the classrooms, common rooms, extra-curricular events or in the political arena, we all learn from one another and everyone has a part to play.

This book introduces the history, activities and people of the Adult Community College, Colchester (known colloquially as 'Grey Friars') which has served local adults from the 1960s to the twenty-first century, and, we hope, will continue to do so for many years to come.

1

The Early History of Grey Friars

Grey Friars is a red brick building in the High Street. Go up the four stone steps to the blue door. Open it and you're inside the Adult Community College, Colchester. It has a warm, friendly atmosphere.

Grey Friars is an odd name for a classic Georgian house. The Reverend Jill Newham's considerable, but unpublished, research on the history of Grey Friars[1], has provided us with a fascinating insight into its history. Once there was a Franciscan friary on this site and the friars wore grey tunics girded with white cords, so were commonly called grey friars. We don't know when the friary was founded, but it certainly existed before January 25th 1279, when Edward I gave the friars a licence to make an underground conduit beneath his land, bringing water from a well or spring that they had been given outside the town. The original friary was probably timber-framed. Edward II gave them more land on which to extend their building, and in 1309 Robert Baron Fitzwalter gave them another half acre, and it was probably here that their church was founded.

Franciscan friars lived according to an ideal of total poverty, aiming to subsist by the labour of their hands and by charitable donations. In 1479 Edward IV gave the friars and their successors fifty-two loads of underwood a year from his forest at Kingswood on the condition that they prayed for the good estate of him and his queen while they were alive, and after death for their souls. Each cartload of wood had to be such as could be pulled by six horses or other beasts. But donations came from more ordinary people too - Alys Cawyston of Tollesbury bequeathed five shillings to the 'graye Fryers off Collchester... to praye For my sowle and all Cristyn sowlys'.

Henry VIII's dissolution of the monasteries in the 1530s led to the site being sold to Francis Jobson, a favoured servant of Henry, and three other men, including the son of the Earl of Leicester and the son of the MP for Essex. Later, Jobson is recorded as owning the four dwellings that comprised the friary, leasing out most of the property, probably himself living in the 'Olde Halle'. He sold it to William Watson, a wool merchant and subsequently the house passed through various hands.

By 1724, when the present central building, the basis of the building that we walk into today, was constructed by Thomas Bayes, it was called Grey Friars House, a clear reference to its origins. Morant, in his 1748 'History and Antiquities of Colchester' recorded it, still under the same name, as belonging to Dr Robert Potter.

Dr Robert Potter (portrait in Colchester Borough Council Museums collection).

In his revised edition of 1768 Morant added, 'Of him it was purchased [in 1752] by the Revd. John Halls, who hath built a very handsome house, and made good gardens, with other improvements.' John Halls, rector of Easthorpe, extended and modernised the house, adding fashionable Georgian details such as the octangular bay windows and the Ionic style surround to the front door. Jill Newham felt that some features suggested it may have been built on the site of a medieval house, possibly the gatehouse to the friary.

After Halls' death the house was put up for auction. The estate agents detailed an attractive building: 'The house is a substantial brick edifice, with a double bowed front, and contains, on the ground story [sic], a neat entrance hall, library, drawing room, breakfast room, capital dining parlour, store room, roomy closets, water closets, &c; 7 airy bedrooms on the first story, with store room, closets, &c. 4 good chambers on the upper story with store-room, closets, &c. The offices comprise excellent kitchen, store closets, servants' hall, bake house, and scullery, pantries, larders, dairy, and roomy cellars in the basement, paved yard, with gates to the street, double coach house with very extensive store chamber over it, and two three-stall stables, brew house, and various outbuildings, all of the most substantial brick, and in perfect repair, lawns and pleasure grounds, fishponds, a capital kitchen garden, partly walled and well stocked with fruit trees, another garden completely walled round, dry gravel walks, productive orchard, farm yard and outbuildings, enclosed by walls.'

The house went on to be occupied by a variety of owners and tenants. Clergymen lived here, an eminent woman brewer, an apothecary, a merchant, a silk throwster and a magistrate. Census returns tell us that in 1841 Grey Friars House was occupied by Charles Bawtree, his twenty-five year old wife Eliza, and their four children, Charles (4), Frederick (3), Arthur (2) and Eliza (1).

The oldest part of Grey Friars might well have become the home of Colchester Royal Grammar School if the latter's trustees had succeeded in their attempts to buy it in the first half of the nineteenth century.

The Colchester and Essex Botanical and Horticultural Society, founded in 1823, took out a twenty-one year lease on the eight and a half acre garden: 'The situation is beautiful, commanding a view of the surrounding country at once varied and extensive, while it is of additional interest to many, that the ancient *Wall* of the town forms its northern and eastern boundary,' says the nineteenth century *History of Colchester*. This garden was very methodical: 'The herbaceous collection will be arranged according to the sexual system of Linnaeus, and the medical plants after his natural method,' says the *History*. There were also fruit trees, forest trees and shrubs, aquatic plants, a greenhouse, a seed-shop and a potting-house. It must have been magnificent. Nevertheless, and in spite of the additional attractions of fireworks, a good brass band, and Mr C Green making a grand ascent 'in his splendid new balloon: "The Royal Victoria and Brunswick", with which he had the honour to convey His Highness the Duke of Brunswick over the British Channel on 31st March 1851,' the botanical garden closed in 1853. Roman Road and Castle Road were built on its site.

In the early twentieth century, conflict between church and state was again responsible for a change in the ownership of Grey Friars. In 1903 the Ladies of Nazareth, a group of nuns driven out of France by the anti-clerical Law of Associations, came via their convent in Ealing to find refuge in Colchester. They bought Hill Crest and Grey Friars, and, having extended it by adding on the wings, which were built by the contractor Robert Beaumont, they opened a girls' school. The nuns belonged to a Franciscan order, as the friars had done. Their convent was called variously the Convent of Nazareth or Grey Friars Convent, according to insurance records. It was lit by electricity, and had a boiler in the basement. Only the lay sisters were allowed out of the building, and the only man allowed in was Dr Nicholson from Gate House. When the nuns were instructing the builders, they had to speak to them through an iron grille.

According to the Colchester Girls' High School minute book of 1956, evidence of the nuns' residence survived in the confessional in the gym cupboard and the holy water basin in one of the cloakrooms. Some features are still in situ in the passages leading to the crèche in Hillcrest. After the First World War the nuns sold their school to Essex Education Committee and returned to France, taking with them all their belongings, which entirely filled two barges at the Hythe. In February 1920 the Franciscans again left Grey Friars.

Colchester County High School

In 1919 the school was housed entirely in the North Hill building, and it was overflowing. 'The staff room was taken over for a form room,' says the hand-written minute book, in an extract entered in 1956, 'there were classes in the corridor, coachings in every corner and even the gallery was used, a wooden trellis being erected to prevent those from above who were more interested in gym than geometry from joining the class below head first!'

The minute book records: 'Great was the relief when the Essex Education Committee took over Grey Friars and it was decided to house the Junior School there, together with Miss Harris and the Preparatory which had hitherto been functioning in St Peter's rooms. During the second half of the autumn term and all through the Easter holidays we worked feverishly under Miss Crosthwaite's lead to get the building furnished and habitable. At last the finishing touches were put and we were ready! Imagine our horror at finding one Monday morning in the first term that the roof was on fire! The telephone had only just been installed and its first call was for the fire brigade which turned out to be a mere handcart and hose. Imagine our dismay when the hose burst in the top corridor and water poured through the ceilings, down the stairs in a torrent and out of the front door. It meant a day's holiday for us and might have meant much more. Face to face with impending disaster we realised as never before what a precious possession Grey Friars was to us.'

Colchester County High School's tenure lasted from the Spring Term 1920 until the end of 1957, and it is remembered by many for the restful charm of its classrooms and garden. However, the division of the school between the Grey Friars and North Hill sites, with no quick communication except through the town's busiest street, was not without its drawbacks. On one occasion, it is recorded, 'we all went down to Grey Friars in a crocodile that stretched nearly from one school to the other'. Most senior girls had to walk to Grey Friars at least twice weekly for Physics, Art, or special coaching.

Miss Crosthwaite feared that separation of the two departments, with no common assembly, would lead to its development into two distinct communities; only her own forceful personality and that of her successor prevented this. She had hoped to see a new building for the seniors erected opposite Grey Friars, but this proved impossible. The accommodation at Grey Friars had been gratefully accepted and soon the junior school was developing its special way of life, with a library and out-of-class activities of its own. This has resonance with the later use of Grey Friars as an adult college, when the extension of the College's activities to include the Wilson Marriage Centre in the 1990s brought the need to ensure that both sites' activities clearly followed the college's overall ethos and philosophy.

Grey Friars created a powerful impression on the schoolgirls. One of them, Mrs C.A. Page, of Clacton, who came to C.C.H.S. in 1925, described it thus: 'Coming from a small village school as a scholarship entrant I was completely overawed by Grey Friars. The main staircase was like one in a country house, and we had to change into "house shoes" of identical pattern when we arrived. Satchels were put into a cupboard and collected when we went home. You were not allowed to run down corridors...

The grounds at the back were spacious and beautiful. There was a lawn dominated by a very large, spreading holm oak tree, and, on a lower level, another lawn with the remains of a conservatory. We weren't allowed to go in as it was unsafe. It was covered in wisteria, beautiful when in bloom. There was a shallow pool on the lawn. One year our French class put on a short version of "Snow White" on the lawn. It came to an abrupt ending when someone fell into the pond and those of us doing the play very self-consciously in French were very glad!

An emphasis was put on music. The school had a music club ... and it was a highlight for me. Beatrix Harrison, who was noted for playing her violin in a nightingale wood for broadcasting came with her sister, May, more than once. Anna Neagle's brother, Stuart Robertson, a very good-looking blond baritone came to Grey Friars, also Keith Faulkner, again very good-looking. It was a job to concentrate on lessons after this. We also had a famous harpist, Marie Korchinska, whose gleaming golden harp and beautiful ball gown were magical.

We had an annual Christmas party when the teaching staff entertained the girls. One year they put on a circus and I was staggered to see staid mistresses jumping through paper hoops! At Christmas in Assembly the school sang "Oh come all ye faithful" in Latin. Those of us learning Latin felt superior using the correct pronunciation! I considered it an excellent school apart from the fact that some fee-paying girls looked down on the scholarship girls, but I think that could happen anywhere.

Before I finish I must mention a "secret" passage which went from the upper floors down a winding staircase, and came out of the panelling near the dining room. It was the thing to do it *once* and appear suddenly in front of those coming out of the dining room! Of course we weren't *supposed* to use it.' (See colour photo section)

Christine Mabbitt, too, had fond memories that she related in a newsletter: 'I was within a few days of being six years old when I started school at Grey Friars. The first form was in Room 13, with its lovely bay window overlooking the lawn. I clearly remember being shown where to put my hat and coat in the cloakroom adjacent, beyond which was a lavatory with an enormous toilet: I was afraid of falling in. All the indoor toilets were wonderful pieces of ceramic with wide wooden seats. Lower 11 was the next form (we did not call them classes), housed underneath room 13, again with a beautiful bay window opening onto the terrace above the lawn.

Classroom 3: in the 1755 extension.

7

'The younger children all had form rooms in the older central part of the building, and I came to love the carved overmantels and the staircase with its graceful handrail. At the beginning of each term we received our new text books (after our parents had perused the list and sent the required money). Form by form we were led up the dark, narrow, twisty stairs, past Room 22, to what were the attics of the old house - dark and creepy. A window looked down on to the first floor landing. By this window stood a horrifying contraption which I now realise was a hoist. There was a low ceilinged room in the centre front of the building, with shelving piled high with books. I still have many of my books including quite a row of Kings Treasury editions and Blackie Plain Text Shakespeares.

One nature study lesson, when I was in the Lower Thirds in Room 12, a teacher took us round the gardens. I had already been most impressed by the winter aconites that covered the ground near the Yew tree at the corner of the playground. Now we were learning the names of the trees. I have always remembered that lesson. The great Holm Oak is still there, some of the Yew trees, the Walnut (then much smaller), the Lime and the Chestnuts. The Eucalyptus seems to have disappeared. The Mulberry fell down in a storm while I was there and the big Beech was removed to make the back entrance of the Clinic. The conservatory with its gigantic, sweet smelling Wisteria went for the same reason.

There was a "Raised Path" between the playground and kitchen garden. The south side of the raised path (very stony: disastrous on knees) contained a glorious herbaceous border with peonies, poppies, lupins and delphiniums. Half way along was a rose-covered pergola with an everlasting pea at its foot - truly everlasting: it is still there. The main kitchen garden, now car-park, I suspect provided the vegetables for our school dinners. There was box edging along all the pathways. Under the high boundary wall to Roman and Castle roads girls interested in gardening had their own plots which they dug and cultivated with enthusiasm during the dinner hour. There was a small pond in the corner of the lower lawn which was home for newts and frogs, and, occasionally, girls who leant over too far.

It was a beautiful place in which to be educated. The atmosphere of the building and the large garden has left an indelible impression. I could go on for hours about the Music Club concerts (once Madame Suggia

The Grey Friars hall in the 1920s.

played for us), about the gym competitions, the sports days and spectaculars staged on the lawn in summer when, as a first former, I and my friends were dressed as daisies to partner the buttercups in Lower 11.'

Sheila Scott, (who, at the time of writing is still involved with Grey Friars as a tutor of choral singing) remembers her school years at Grey Friars like this: 'My first trip to Grey Friars was in 1941 when I sat my 11-plus examination there. Two things stick in my mind – the mini-bar of Cadbury's chocolate we were each given afterwards and the little ivory and ebony 'eye' in the banister rail newel post – which is still there!

The years I spent at Grey Friars in the junior department of the County High School for Girls were such happy ones. Until recently the classrooms changed little and I was almost certainly taught in every one of them at one time or another. When we reached the top form, we were sometimes asked to supervise the preparatory class while they played in the wisteria-hung arbour at the far end of the lawn – also no more and now part of the overflow car park. Their classroom was room one – still one of the most pleasant in the building.

Today, the Hall hasn't changed at all, except for the removal of the gymnastic wall bars. We had assembly there every day and I still recall thumping out "Lili Marlene" on the piano.' Sheila returned to Grey Friars as a music student in the 1960s. The building was temporarily a base for the music department of the rapidly expanding North East Essex Technical College and School of Art (now Colchester Institute). Her husband Don remembers impressive photos in a local newspaper capturing the scene when the pianos were removed from the top floor by crane.

The High School regretfully left Grey Friars when it moved to Norman Way, but everyone was glad to know that its heavy front door still welcomed scholars to its congenial rooms and splendid gardens.

A stroll around Grey Friars in the twenty-first century provides some notable contrasts to the world described above, but still echoes the thirst for knowledge. "Admission free – all welcome" proclaims the poster advertising the Film Club's first showing of 2005, "Buongiorno, notte", an Italian film with English subtitles. Other linguistic delights in prospect include films in Mandarin, Dutch, Chilean, Russian and, of course, German and French.

The entrance hall's illuminated display cabinet draws attention to the College's information technology programme with the exhibit "The way we were – the way we are now". A 'Royal' sit-up-and-beg typewriter, accompanied by a combined type-cleaning brush/eraser, sits next to a leviathan Burroughs calculating machine – all in sharp contrast to, and dwarfing, the tiny silicon chips and neat circuits on the displayed 'mother board' from a standard desktop computer. The description of the array of programmes and functions such a small object can operate is breathtaking.

[MF]

Reference

1   Newham, Rev Jill (1986) *Notes and files on the history of Grey Friars* (unpublished) in Grey Friars Archives, currently held by CALCAG's publishing division – Access Books, Colchester

The Holm Oak 2004

The soft grey leaves of the holm oak hang over the car park like a shadow, a ghost. The great branches stretch their dark limbs to the clouds; they yawn wide. The leaves hang down, they whisper.

This was my garden, they mourn over the lost roses, the lost lawns, the lost children, the lost rustle of long skirts. This was my garden.

Gone is the softness of reflections in a water-lilied pond, the small frog poised forever to jump at its edge. Just the raw metallic curves of Ford and Vauxhall now, Honda and Toyota and the rest in rows now. The sun glints sharp on their windscreens. The smell drifts of petrol and diesel. This was my garden, the holm oak mourns.

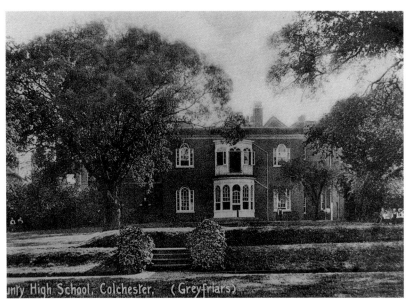

A 1920s view from the gardens. Holm oak on left of picture.

The roof is a rhythm of slopes, plains and ridges, up and down it goes, up and down restlessly. Old tiles, that beautiful soft red, are gilt and grayed with lichen. The lead has recently been renewed, and is gaunt, held on with clips. Chimney pots – count them as you stand outside room 26 – four, five, ten, fourteen – can you see more?

The dome above the stairwell bursts like a bubble through a flat roof that when you try to make sense of all the complexity you think must surely be a late addition.

The roof is a stillness caught in the rocking of the green treetops, the sweep of clouds across the sky, a scrap of blue.

<>

A corridor in one of the French nuns' wings.

A pleat of brown carpet, beige walls, white sash windows.

The raw utilitarian strip lights that permeate this place assert relentlessly, they won't let you forget, this is a school. We are serious here.

18, 19 up above the doors like lift numbers. The same odd mix of new and old that's everywhere: a filing cabinet next to a lino-topped wooden cupboard that must surely date from the days here of the County High School. Green fire exit signs, steps up to where varnished boards gleam under the electric light.

Two wooden tables stretch out against the wall, their dark surfaces scored with ink and scratches, years of wear.

<>

The stairs curl up out of the hall.

The banisters gleam, smoothed by hundreds of years of hands stroking them. Family hands; little children, grandparents, aunts and uncles.

Schoolgirls.

The banisters are smoothed by years of happiness and fears.

Cloud-light falls on the stairs at the core of the house through the glass dome above, like a blessing.

Maggie Freeman

2

Adult Education in Essex

There was, of course, adult education in Essex long before the present adult college was developed at Grey Friars. In common with many communities throughout the country, there were adult learning activities for a variety of purposes - from teaching people to read the Bible to the efforts of philanthropists to encourage and assist the working classes to better themselves. Churches were once a great provider of education for the poor, with people keen to hear, and learn to read, the first printed translation of the Bible into English. Such education was often for very specific outcomes, as made clear by a vicar in neighbouring Kent who saw its purpose ' ... to be taught to read and be instructed in the plain duties of the Christian religion, with a particular view to their good and industrious behaviour in their future character of labourers and servants.' Nonconformist ministers were, however, to take a wider view of the purposes of education - to enable working people to improve themselves and their position in society.[1]

By the nineteenth century, however, both Anglicans and nonconformists supported the movement to set up Mechanics' Institutes and this was very enthusiastically taken up in Essex. The institutes, along with the University Settlements (which took learning out into the heart of communities) were perhaps the nearest to the Grey Friars experience of today. Two of the earliest, those in Colchester and Chelmsford, were founded in 1833. Other towns soon followed suit, sometimes forming Literary Institutes or Mutual Improvement Societies.

Colchester Mechanics' Institute was 'for the promulgation of useful knowledge among all persons, but more especially the working classes'.[2] It received large subscriptions from Whig gentlemen and was soon able to hire premises in which to hold lectures, keep a library and provide newspapers and magazines. There were classes in English, geography and arithmetic. The diaries of prominent nineteenth century Colcestrians, especially the 'self-made men' William Wire (watchmaker and antiquarian) and William

Castle (silk weaver and the first manager of the Colchester Cooperative Society) give a very clear picture of the need to make up for a lack of education. Castle noted, upon being passed over for a post as foreman, 'When I think of the narrow escape I had for want of education I am forced to be a strong advocate for compulsory education.' [3] This was in 1850 and education was not to be made compulsory until 1876.

Because the Mechanics' Institute was alleged to have political leanings, in 1849 a rival Colchester Literary Institute was founded. By 1851 the latter had 384 members, including a group which later became the Essex Archaeological Society. Fortnightly lectures were held between September and April (which remains the peak season for adult classes, although fourth term 'Summer Schools' and 'drop-in' IT centres have begun the move towards year-long adult education activities).

In 1859 the Mechanics' Institute in Colchester fell into debt and was dissolved. The Literary Institute seems to have closed before 1903.

At Chelmsford Mechanics' Institute the fortnightly lectures were very popular in the late 1800s, with attendance sometimes exceeding 400. But what in the long term proved most in demand at all the institutes were the libraries and the reading rooms, which provided facilities that did not exist elsewhere. Another popular attraction generally was the 'spirited entertainment' of Penny Readings.

Most of the Institutes folded because of financial problems. One of those that survived the longest was the Saffron Walden Literary and Scientific Institute, which was still going strong in 1954, with about 370 members. In the 1960s it was made over to Essex County Council as a charitable trust, and metamorphosed into the Victorian Studies Centre – it has a huge collection of rare Victorian books. True to its old tradition, it still gives three lectures a year.

In 1859 there was an evening school for females in Coggeshall, and there were plans to open one for boys. In Colchester, the Co-operative Society opened an education centre at its Culver Street assembly rooms and in 1894 commercial classes were started for members' sons. Wilson Marriage started an elementary adult school for men for the Society of Friends at their East Stockwell Street meeting house. Their provision was enhanced by a Sunday school for females circa 1871 and following a successful decade and a move to the new meeting house at Sir Isaac's Walk, a dedicated schoolroom was built. Following a downturn in support, the education programme had declined by the early 1900s.

In 1885 James Paxman was a leading presence in the setting up of the Albert School of Science and Art, comprising day and evening classes for adults in the old corn exchange. Two years later, whilst mayor, Paxman organised the finance to buy the building and convert it for the school and, from 1889, for the new university extension classes from Cambridge. Consolidation and expansion of the school, a tenure in North Hill and a move to Sheepen Road resulted in the present Colchester Institute, which still numbers many adults in its student body.

By 1904 Colchester Borough Education Committee was providing evening continuation classes at North Street School in subjects such as writing, arithmetic, book-keeping, needlework, French and physical exercises. Then in the 1960s Colchester Senior Evening Institute was founded, with an initial intake of 248 students: by 1972 there were 5,963 enrolments, clear proof of the demand for provision of adult education.

From the 1970s there was a raised awareness of the need to widen participation for certain groups: the unemployed, those in need of basic skills, women returners, volunteers and parents, but because these types of course are more expensive to run in terms of staff and daytime accommodation, the Essex curriculum tended to be more traditional, even into the eighties. In September 1982 the categories of courses provided Essex-wide were as follows (with the Essex and Grey Friars 2004 figures for comparison):

Category	Essex 1982	Essex 2004	Grey Friars 2004
Creative / aesthetic	32%	15%	21%
Health / physical	23%	14%	18%
Intellectual / scientific / technical	13%	3%	4%
Languages	12%	12%	10%
Vocational (mainly office skills)	8%	21%	21%
Civic (eg volunteers, parenting)	4%	13%	8%
Basic (eg literacy & numeracy)	3%	23%	18%

In 1982 28% of Essex courses were run in the daytime, 72% in the evening. By 2004 Grey Friars had 69% daytime, 31% evening.

Statistics need to be treated with caution. For example, some of the differences reflect changes in definition of purpose rather than subject category. IT-based courses which may have been originally designated 'scientific' are now mostly categorised as 'vocational' due to the national shift in IT applications.

Also, this chart is based on numbers of courses rather than amount of time given to courses. If time is used as a measure, for example, Grey Friars' basic skills contribution rises to 27% and languages to 19% whereas creative drops to 19% and health / physical to 12%. Also, the low percentage in the 'civic' category does not do justice to Grey Friars' comprehensive 'outreach' programme as many of these activities have not registered on the official statistics.

Nevertheless, the chart does point to a significant shift in curriculum towards vocational subjects and the allied basic skills. Grey Friars can be seen to reflect the Essex trend, modified slightly by its preservation of a greater number of creative and health-related courses.

In 1990 the Conservative government's "Further and Higher Education Act" produced a new quango - the Further Education Funding Council (FEFC). It set out to revolutionise the post-school education sector by taking FE away from the control of the local education authorities (LEAs) run by local councils and setting up a 'new sector' comprising Further Education (FE) 'corporations' – being the former LEA FE colleges re-designated as separate non-commercial companies running their own affairs. Funding for this sector was put in the hands of a new Further Education Funding Council, and cash was only available directly to the new 'incorporated' bodies, or indirectly to other bodies 'sponsored' by the FE colleges. This caused repercussions throughout the country for the providers of 'traditional' adult education – for, with a few exceptions, they were excluded from the new sector. In Colchester, the Colchester Institute and the Sixth Form College were 'incorporated' and began running themselves, independently of the LEA, but Grey Friars was designated as an 'external institution', remaining under the control of Essex County Council.

The LEA did eventually strengthen their adult education service by combining all provision in each of 12 districts under 11 'adult community colleges' and one adult residential college (Wansfell College, in Theydon Bois, on the perimeter of Epping Forest). Grey Friars, as the base for the

Adult Community College, Colchester, responded with enthusiasm to its new responsibilities and rapidly established a local, regional and national reputation for a wide curriculum, high academic standards, interaction with the local community and highly-qualified staff.

When the government changed political colour in 1997, there were many adjustments to the national system of post-school education, but along with greater financial commitment came an 'audit culture' which, far from dealing with many of the problems from the previous administration, in fact produced a plethora of paper-work, checks and inspections.

In 2004, largely in response to the mechanistic demands of the FEFC's replacement, the Learning and Skills Council (LSC) and the new Adult Learning Inspectorate (ALI), Essex County Council's management of the LEA's adult education service (to which Grey Friars still belonged) took a turn towards centralisation. Wansfell College was closed and options for future plans were being discussed, including the possibility of either full centralisation, the introduction of 'contracting-out' provision and/or merging the nine separate and distinctive adult community colleges into a smaller number.

And so adult education pursued an uneven course, responding to government directives, availability of funding, the needs of the responsible public bodies – and all the while striving to make its curriculum and organisation relevant to local communities. In Colchester, between 1997 and 2000 Grey Friars analysed and reviewed its curriculum to take account of the Government's requirement for more skills-related learning opportunities. This did not lead to radical changes as the curriculum already had opportunities for progression to higher levels in the majority of subjects. What it did require, however, was a clear strategy to ensure that the non-accredited courses were protected from decline as they became starved of funding. Managers introduced a budgeting system which, for the time being, was to cross-subsidise such courses, first, to protect entry points for people with no previous experience and, second, to continue higher-level, but unexamined, courses to cater for those who wanted to progress further, but did not need qualifications. The comprehensive nature of the curriculum was thus preserved for the foreseeable future.

Why is Grey Friars so important to the community that it serves? Because it is there as a result of strategic development - not whimsy - and because it is consistent in providing the opportunity for high quality learning experiences. Opportunities which adults can access at times that fit in with the muddled lives that most of us lead; juggling work and family commitments, caring for young children or the elderly, coping with shocks like redundancy, retirement and bereavement.

The importance of this accessibility can not be overstated. The fact that Grey Friars is here to provide unquestioning support. The fact that it provides breadth of opportunity and social equality - it values everyone.

[MF]

References

1   Fieldhouse, Roger and associates (1996) *A History of Modern British Adult Education* NIACE, Leicester

2   Cromwell, Thomas, (1825) *History and Description of the Ancient Borough of Colchester in Essex - volumes I and II* Jennings, Poultry

3   Brown, A.F.J., (1972) *Essex People 1750 - 1900 from their diaries, memoirs and letters* Essex County Council, Chelmsford

3

A College for Adults

People of all ages can access much of the further and higher education provided mainly for younger people and in many cases they are positively welcomed. The new technologies offer on-line learning, now possible virtually anywhere. However, it is overwhelmingly still the case that the majority of adults wish to learn in the company of people with whom they feel comfortable. These two students, 30 years apart in age, featured on the latest College video.

Darien said, 'When I started out in September I was just expecting it to be a course so I could fill my time and it turned out to be something I really enjoyed ... around November/December time I was ready to do Maths GCSE ... I thought this was going to be the first thing I successfully have got myself and even thinking about it cheered me up so much, I thought "one step forward". It does help when you can feel as comfortable as if you are sitting in a front room with your friends, because that is what it is basically and I am looking forward to it - and if I can get there early on I turn up earlier'.

Marion said: 'I retired from private practice as a solicitor about 18 months ago, I'd had enough, and I needed to change. So I spent about a year wondering what I was going to do, and saw an advertisement ... Until then I hadn't even considered adult community education. It's something that when you've been 'educated', you've had your education throughout your life, you've been a professional, you don't automatically think of as a way of changing the direction of your life. The standard of tuition here is really high, and it's a nice informal atmosphere, you don't feel inhibited or intimidated by it, because again, there is a sense of partnership and we are here to achieve a common goal, and having an access to education throughout your life I think is very important, because you can always learn new skills ... Again, it's having that goal, having that ambition, and it doesn't stop just because you happen to have attained a certain age, you've still got more ambitions, you've still got other things you want to do'.

If we are to ensure everyone can share Darien and Marion's experiences of a learning environment where 'you feel as comfortable as if you are sitting in a front room with your friends' where 'it's a nice informal atmosphere, you don't feel inhibited or intimidated by it' and 'there is a sense of partnership' we would surely be arguing for a secure and identifiable 'base' for adult learning in every major centre of population.

The stories of how such centres of learning originally came about are many and varied as described by Michael Newman in his 1979 study of adult education 'The Poor Cousin' [1].

He wrote, 'Adult education centres come in all shapes and sizes, based on whatever accommodation they have been given or have managed to scrounge ...' Grey Friars, this book's inspiration, fits this category to some extent. We have its first principal to thank for that. Allin Coleman was the head of the 'Senior Evening Institute' based in one of the town's schools. The need for daytime accommodation meant that he set his sights on space within a semi-redundant school – Grey Friars.

What started as somewhere for an office began to be used for daytime as well as evening classes – when the accommodation and resources could be secured in competition with the daytime requirements of the school. After the new schools were established in their new accommodation, the adult education service spread throughout the building (the habitable parts in the first instance).

Newman described some centres as 'developing in various directions according to the dictates of their areas and their resources and the particular interests and eccentricities of their heads of centre.'

In Colchester, the occupation of Grey Friars became permanent, largely through the tenacity, perseverance and professionalism of the first principal, and "Grey Friars" came to life as a brand name for adult learning in the area. That the ethos created thirty years ago is still as relevant today is testimony to Allin Colemen's clarity of philosophy and foresight. We look at Allin's establishment of Grey Friars as an adult college later in this chapter.

From the time it was owned by the Colchester Borough Education Committee, through to the present day under Essex County Council's ownership, Grey Friars has been the headquarters for the area's main provider of adult education for over thirty years. There have, however, been different official titles over the decades.

'Colchester Senior Evening Institute' reflected its beginnings as an after-school service. 'Colchester Adult Education Centre' with its later addition of the plural to 'Centres' showed its development as an all-day service in an increasing number of venues throughout the town. The present official title 'Adult Community College, Colchester' came into use following the LEA's reorganisation of youth and adult services in the early 1990s when all adult education services in Essex were re-established as Adult Community Colleges. The new local college covered the whole borough, incorporating the programmes run in Tiptree, Wivenhoe and other venues outside the town, but remained based at Grey Friars.

Throughout its existence, however, no matter what the official title has been, 'Grey Friars' has remained the trade name for adult learning in Colchester. People have been heard to say "I go to a Grey Friars class at Alderman Blaxill School" or more recently "I went to a Grey Friars class in Tiptree last year." Therefore, the term 'Grey Friars' is used interchangeably throughout this book and can mean the building, any adult education activity provided from there, the college as a whole, or, more importantly, the adult learning ethos as exemplified by the college's students, staff and governors.

The genesis of the college's second site, the Wilson Marriage Centre, is a perfect example of the interface between politics and community learning – and it starts with a Grey Friars connection.

Twenty years after the transformation of Grey Friars from a school to the town's home of adult learning, a 'review of assets' carried out by County Council officials, mooted a merger onto one site of Colchester's youth services, community and adult education and the youth training scheme.

One element of this 'tidying-up' exercise would be the closure of Grey Friars and the selling-off of the property. Three sites were used by various branches of the County Council's Community Education Service at the time. Brooklands was a large house in its own grounds in Brook Street; East Ward the site of a closed school and Grey Friars was the third main site. The Wilson Marriage School had also closed and its main building had been renovated following a serious fire and officials took the view that all three services could move in together in the refurbished school, allowing the County Council to sell off the three vacated sites.

One County Hall officer, when told that the Grey Friars adult education programme would not fit into the Wilson Marriage premises suggested the problem could be solved by building a new 'adult wing' to increase the space, but everyone knew that would only happen provided extra money was made available. Another officer was told that closure of Grey Friars would not be a popular move and he was warned of the likely public outcry. His response was categorical: 'That's no problem - there's no constituency for adult education!'

However the officials did not get their way. A hue and cry was raised by adult students past and present and Grey Friars stayed as it was. Brooklands and East Ward closed and amalgamated in Wilson Marriage School. Later, the youth training scheme having closed and the youth service having reorganised and left the site, the Wilson Marriage Centre for Community Education has not replaced Grey Friars, but has joined it as part of the Adult Community College serving the borough.

During another discussion about possible reorganisation of adult education services, an LEA official said, 'Adult education would be better off being completely spread out throughout communities.' This echoes Newman's observation that, 'Some "centres" may have no centre at all but consist of a scatter of classes, sponsored by the WEA together with a university, say, and housed in clubs, community centres and church halls in a number of villages dotted around a market town'.

Such provision has been criticised as being rather insular and self-serving, thus not deserving of public funding, but more recently activities of this kind have been recognised as enhancing the menu of opportunities. Whether through classes and events at local community-based venues, or by using a travelling classroom with its own power supply and facilities, learning provided in the heart of communities has been accepted as a way of encouraging adults to return to learning.

But what such localised provision cannot do is create an identifiable and secure community of learners. Rather, if they remain isolated and disconnected from other educational provision, they are often in danger of contributing to the argument that says that public education funds are not best used in supporting the existence of isolated interest groups.

The 'Grey Friars' way of making coherent a mix of centralised and local provision is to take responsibility for ensuring that there is a balance of opportunities throughout the area. Local opportunities should relate strategically to the whole programme and as a result enhance the comprehensive nature of what could be termed an 'area curriculum'. Resources can be deployed where they can be most effective.

It is in this respect that being part of a local authority can be useful in maximising the effectiveness of scarce resources. Sharing strategies with those responsible for planning other services (such as transport, social services, health, housing and other facets of local regeneration and development) enables agencies to avoid working in isolation - possibly inadvertently duplicating others' efforts. Otherwise, the link with the LEA can be just about control and auditing activities - characterised by increasing bureaucracy and lack of local autonomy and relevance.

On the latest college video[2], a parent tells how successful such collaboration can be when all goes smoothly. In this case the adult college worked with a local County primary school, the Borough Council and a local charitable body.

'At the school my son goes to (on the St. Anne's estate) they advertised Grey Friars courses starting actually at the school. It was a 'Word Power' course, which involves Basic English, with your children coming to the class with you, and I thought maybe I could start refreshing my memory on things and get more qualifications behind me in order actually to get back to the world and work. Doing the first two courses at the school gave me the confidence to go on and do a creative writing course. I am also doing a parenting course, which is run by the social services and helps you deal with teenagers.' She continues, smiling, 'I have got so much more confidence I am also now a parent governor at my son's school, and I stick up for myself more now. Most of all, the education was fun. It wasn't hard, it wasn't impossible and the tutors made it so easy for us to learn that we were like little sponges sucking out all the knowledge that we could - and there are a lot of like-minded people out there.'

She concludes, 'There are a few of us who now have gone out and started a parents' group for the estate, where we are getting them to come in and help with the children, so in a way they are self-educating as well. It's getting better, we have an Association now, for which I am the secretary and we are getting together as a community. It is exactly what it needs: it needs input of money from the Council and it needs education.'

There is no point in designing a comprehensive curriculum if the student body turns out to be anything but representative of the local community. And if the whole offer is based around activities in a building which appears to be exclusive and forbidding to those with less than positive prior experiences of education there is only one outcome, as Helena Kennedy noted in her report Learning Works: 'If at first you don't succeed – you don't succeed.'

There are many heart-warming stories from those who successfully combated literacy and / or numeracy problems and many concern 'the big blue door' – the High Street entrance to Grey Friars. After they have coped with the hard work of study, the struggle to pass through the 'learning plateau' reached after a rapid and rewarding start to a programme – even the difficulties of time and money – many say they recognise that entering the big blue front door was a significant event in their lives. Some of these stories are told in chapter 6.

Imposingly built, like so many Georgian town-house front doors, large enough to allow a sedan chair through to its impressive hallway, the door formed, for Grey Friars' earlier tenants, a solid barrier to the world beyond.

This barrier is now, of course, more psychological than physical, but the significance of a symbol such as a door should never be underestimated. Grey Friars staff have worked hard to ensure that the door is perceived as the entrance to a world of opportunities – the start of a journey during which more doors will be opened through learning.

From the beginning of Grey Friars' development as a college for adults, rather than simply a 'night school', 'evening institute' or 'adult education centre' there has been a desire within its management to aim for not only a high-quality educational establishment, but also somewhere where local people feel welcome and involved. Grey Friars was one of the first such establishments under local authority control to have a members' association, significant student representation on the advisory and governing bodies, a range of self-governing clubs and societies springing from its educational activities, and targeted activities aimed at tackling exclusion.

But, however useful such strategies may be, there is a more fundamental need: for people who attend to be well taught, motivated, even empowered and enthused by tutors who not only know their subjects, but love them and enjoy sharing their expertise. There is no better way to advertise the value of learning than to give people positive, enjoyable experiences. They will then become advocates, as has been proved by the increasing involvement of what the authorities term 'non-traditional users' and 'reluctant learners'. It has not been the increased availability of funds which has opened doors to the wider population, but good, strategic use of those funds within an ethos of lifelong learning for all.

The rapid development of IT has given the world of education a new resource. Adult educators have readily accepted the flexibility given by the new technologies, but believe that it takes its place in a wide range of approaches and cannot itself revolutionise learning. They are sceptical of the alacrity with which government agencies have seized upon IT as a way of 'increasing participation'.

'The LSC is committed to making full and effective use of e-learning in strengthening the quality, accessibility and relevance of the learning we fund. We are developing e-skills and promoting e-learning as a critical means of extending participation, so that all young people and adults are provided with opportunities to learn and develop their skills throughout their working lives.' Thus states the Learning & Skills Council Corporate Plan[3] for the period to the end of 2006.

Whilst colleges have embraced the IT revolution in the widest sense, enhancing their curricula accordingly, many IT-dedicated 'learning centres' have arrived in a blaze of hype, free offers and prize draws. Unfortunately, many of these centres have a limited range of opportunities, often cherry-picked from an already well-established range of courses.

If, however, their contribution forms part of a strategically-planned curriculum, the comprehensive offer is of course enhanced by the adoption of the latest electronic gadgetry. A range of courses and activities, on and off site, on the road, or to be followed at home via internet connections, can, of course, increase choice and opportunity for prospective learners.

But IT should not stand alone. IT does not provide a single solution to the problem of addressing the wide range of adult learning needs, complicated as it is by its relevance both to the nation's economic and social requirements and the need to address individuals' readiness to learn.

What is needed is a comprehensive system to deliver a comprehensive curriculum. Adult learning needs a strong and identifiable base, not only as its strategic centre, but also as a core focus to exemplify what the whole service means throughout the community.

Grey Friars is that solid core in the local context. The College's influence emanates from there. With Grey Friars as the flagship of a fleet of opportunities including activities in village halls, local schools, in a travelling classroom and on companies' premises, there can be local coherence in the learning programme. With Grey Friars staff participating in, and sometimes leading, co-operative ventures with other educational providers, borough and parish councils, regional and national government and local and national advocacy groups there can be a co-ordinated rather than, at best, a scattergun approach – and at worst, naked competition in the pursuance of targeted funding to increase a provider's individual profile.

But Grey Friars (or a similar institution anywhere) is not able to do any of this unless it achieves recognition and becomes significant not only in the eyes of the local people, but also within the local educational, social and political environment.

In order to achieve this, a 'Grey Friars' anywhere has to be allowed to develop according to local requirements (albeit within a national funding context and strategies of its 'owners' eg LEA or charity). It must also ensure it engages with its local communities and that it develops its managers and staff at the same time as it develops as an institution.   [AS]

Allin Coleman – the first Grey Friars principal

As explained earlier, Grey Friars was used by the County as temporary accommodation for the new secondary schools being built to serve the expansion of Colchester. One school was Monkwick Secondary (now Thomas, Lord Audley) and one of the teachers there was the young, idealistic and enthusiastic Allin Coleman. He already knew of Grey Friars as a result of his marriage to Brenda in 1959. Brenda had been a pupil at the County High School for Girls when it was based in Grey Friars and remembers the delightful kitchen gardens supplying fresh fruit and vegetables for school meals.

Allin had moved to Colchester in the mid 1950s from the West Country where he had gained his first experience of adult education as warden of Brynmawr Community Centre. But he believes his preparation for this role started many years earlier. As a boy of sixteen he used to go to the weekly meeting of the Wesley Guild held in the village Methodist Church his family attended. There, some sixty years ago, he listened to visiting speakers many of whom were skilled at engaging and sharing with others their own learning through judicious use of questions and answers and small-group discussions. 'No one was put down or made to feel their questions were naïve, or laughed at; on the contrary, they were encouraged,' he says.

Looking back, Allin describes this as a 'wonderful learning experience,' and one which had enormous influence on his own intellectual development. It also led to his growing belief in the 'less formal' education of adults. This was the mode of learning which not only fascinated him, but which ultimately enticed him away from his job at Barclays Bank to qualify as a teacher en route to his life-long career in the education of adults.

In Colchester there were no evening classes for adults in 1960, but the Borough Education Officer (Colin Cooper) had seen adult education at work in his native Yorkshire and was anxious to see it happen. His advertisement for a part-time principal to initiate this facility based at the Alderman Blaxill Secondary School immediately attracted Allin, who was the successful candidate.

But of course he still had to keep his day job. During the day he was Senior Master with additional responsibility for careers guidance and for three evenings a week he was the principal of the new adult education provision. He had enjoyed the challenge of setting up the careers service at the school and even more when he extended it into a new, practical 'career-tasting' programme – a forerunner of what was later to become known as 'work experience'. This led to annual 'careers conventions' and even tested the ability of the system to cope with innovation, as the LEA had to address the legal implications of pupils being allowed to leave school without direct teacher supervision. More importantly, it provided experience in extending the boundaries of the education system – a valuable precursor to building a successful community education service.

So, in addition to his main role, how did Allin set about building Colchester's first Senior Evening Institute?

He went to head teachers, negotiated the use of classrooms, about which teachers were often very possessive, and initially invited members of the teaching staff to apply to tutor the adult classes. He then drew up a list of about a dozen classes that he felt he could confidently offer for the first year with a small team of dedicated teachers. Then he toured the town putting up cyclostyled advertisements in shop windows. These were headed Senior Evening Institute. Seeing them strategically placed provided the first tangible evidence that, after all the preparation – and despite the doubts about 'a possible white elephant' raised by some councillors – the vision was finally being realised.

He did, however, have much support for this shared vision from the originator, Colin Cooper, and this support was to grow more tangible as success followed. He had an initial target figure of 250 enrolments, which he feared might be a little over-optimistic. However, on the first evening 248 people registered. Allin described himself that night as being 'absolutely over the moon'! As the term progressed more and more people arrived and additional part-time clerical staff were engaged, courtesy of the Borough Education Officer, to cope with the continual influx.

Having started as a 'one-man-band' (supported willingly and voluntarily by Brenda) as assistance from administrative staff grew, so did Allin's appreciation of the quality and dedication of their contribution. Not only did they do their jobs very well indeed, but they were willing to take responsibility and work out the best way of serving the public. He particularly remembers the selfless dedication of Valerie Denniss and Yvonne Carter, both of whom stayed on, through further decades of struggle and development until their retirements. Such loyalty and hard work combined has been the hallmark of administrative support to subsequent principals. Alan Skinner has told us that this lasts through to the present day, now including reception staff, car park attendants and caretakers as making important contributions to the face-to-face relationships with local people.

Perhaps this proves that where the adult education environment exemplifies the best of the sector's philosophies (such as realising potential, encouraging participation and development, supporting the taking of responsibility) this ethos permeates the whole organisation – and it is not just the students who can learn and develop, it is everyone involved.

In response to the increasing demand, more teachers were employed and additional classes set up, as term by term and year by year the number of enrolments increased. History has shown us that the 1950s and 1960s marked a very significant period of progress in the development of adult learning across the country. Allin was later to be contacted by the National Institute for Adult Education (now NIACE) to be told that Colchester had been identified as the fastest-growing adult education service in the country – its growth rate outstripping the better-resourced towns and cities. Quite understandably, when asked to contribute to research to analyse this phenomenon, he had to decline – his time had to be used *doing* it, rather than analysing it. Here is a link with the modern era that will be recognised and appreciated by the present senior managers. Allin did invite national institute staff to come and see for themselves, however.

Some three years after its inauguration, the Senior Evening Institute headquarters were housed in the partially-vacant premises of Grey Friars and Allin became the first full-time principal. Philip Morant School were still in temporary occupation for a further year and Allin recalls instances where he and the headmaster competed in chess-like manoeuvres over the use of precious teaching space and resources. They were, however, to become good friends and work co-operatively for the benefit of both generations.

The perception and image of Grey Friars was important to Allin and he was determined that, as head, he would be both visible to the members (a warmer word than students) and also to the staff and visiting members of the public. He demonstrated this in four particular ways.

First, he chose the room nearest the front door as his office. Then he aimed to complete his daily administrative duties by 11.30 in order to be free to visit classes, talk to members of staff informally and generally get on with what he describes as 'the real work'. Additionally, he would ensure that he was seldom seen carrying papers or files which he believed would relay the message that he was too busy to be approached. Finally, he made it a habit to be in the vicinity of the exit doors at the end of sessions to bid members farewell as they left the building. Trying to maintain these simple procedures as often as possible, he firmly asserted, was 'time well spent'.

As Grey Friars became more widely known and respected by the local population, it was possible to respond to their stated needs outside the main curriculum. A notable example being the response to police needs to communicate with the influx of foreign juggernaut drivers. A negotiated syllabus, flexible student-orientated timetabling and work-related learning resulted – 40 years in advance of the FEFC, TECs and the LSC and the era of overt government influence on work-related learning!

Allin also wished to raise professional standards. There was little training available for staff for working in adult education then. One could study for diplomas in the broader aspects of the subject at Nottingham and Manchester universities, however, and Allin spent much of his free time studying at Nottingham. The North East Essex Technical College (now the Institute) in Colchester offered a City & Guilds training course for its own staff and Allin worked with them to produce an adult education module suitable for the Grey Friars staff.

It was necessary to support staff in this way, especially when so many were not orientated to adults' learning needs despite being proven craftspeople or school teachers. 'A good teacher is a good teacher,' he says quite sincerely, 'but a teacher of children is not necessarily a good teacher of adults – and of course vice versa.' Allin pays respect to the many senior members of school staff who not only helped him establish adult education courses, but also assisted in converting many people into good teachers of adults. 'Douglas Broom and Norman Curd were the first of many first-class deputies,' he said and gave a further example of Miss Kernahan, a local primary headteacher, who supported a valuable in-service training exercise looking at transferable teaching methods.

Allin was determined that his tutors should develop appropriate methods in their classes. 'At that time many school teachers adopted 'pedagogy' as their (teacher-centred) approach,' he says, 'whereas in helping adults to learn, 'andragogy' (a student-focused perspective) can be more appropriate and successful for both teacher and learners'.[4]

Present principal Alan Skinner was later often to be heard on the occasion of September's 'Preparation Days' cajoling tutors to: 'Think of yourselves less as teachers and more as organisers of other people's learning. You have some knowledge that they need, of course, but you never know who you've got in your class and their motivations for being there until you get to know them. You may be surprised and humbled – so don't set yourselves apart from your students; don't assume you have all the knowledge. Approach your "teaching" as a co-operative activity, where you have the great responsibility to see that everyone, including yourself, learns from the experience.' A clear connection with Allin's assertion that, 'The good teacher of adults learns how to identify and draw upon everyone's knowledge and experience in the context of the subject being studied.'

Allin was also aware of the needs of women who wanted to return to work after having children and who had limited time to study during the day. To enable this to happen, it was necessary to provide equipment such as typewriters (school resources being used in the daytime) and a crèche with trained nursery nurses needed to be set up. As a canteen could not be publicly funded, he financed it initially out of his own pocket, eventually getting refunded. He wanted to offer pottery but had no kiln: the Borough Engineer helped him round that problem.

Allin was most complimentary about the support he received from the Colchester Borough Authority. At that time, in common with Southend, Colchester (in its status as an 'excepted district') retained a considerable measure of power and responsibility over educational matters in its area. 'Next door to us we had the Borough Education Office and a short step up the road was the Borough Treasurer, then the Borough Surveyor and the buildings maintenance departments. I could easily speak with or meet personally any Borough officer – within minutes if really necessary.' Equally important, of course for the local authority, as they were able to experience at first hand the service offered to the public on their behalf. No need, in such a situation, for much of the monitoring paperwork and procedures in evidence today – and much less chance of the Borough officers being accused of faceless bureaucracy.

Some of the courses that Grey Friars introduced at the time were aimed at giving opportunities to people who would not otherwise have had them, so addressing social inequality – and addressing a common criticism of adult education, that it panders to the already-educated middle classes. He also ensured that all households received a prospectus by direct delivery. It is a credit to Allin and his supportive colleagues and staff that many of these programmes and approaches have endured through 40 years of changing times – not due to an unwillingness to develop, but conversely as a result of the core ethos and philosophies being sustainable, continually relevant and adaptable across the decades.

Allin left Grey Friars for Chelmsford in 1974. In a local government reorganisation he was to become the Community Education Officer for Central Essex. In 1979 he returned to university life as Senior Research Fellow to conduct a national survey on retirement and redundancy provision in England and Wales. 'This had a very specific connection with adult education,' he said, 'especially when I joined the Open University to prepare a distance learning course called "Planning Retirement". This was followed by an invitation to set up the Centre for Health and Retirement Education for London University's Birkbeck College in the department headed by Prof Brian Groombridge. This was a great honour.' Allin's research and publications in this field were eventually to become nationally and internationally significant.

The call of Grey Friars was, however, still very strong so when he retired in the early nineties he headed back, suitably disguised as a student in sweater and jeans, to learn basic computer skills and how to enjoy watercolour painting.

He knows Grey Friars has moved on, and he is emotionally detached enough to be pleased about that. 'The proof of what I believed in was that the organisation is bigger than the individual,' he says, stepping back. 'No individual makes a successful organisation on their own. Grey Friars is a prime example of an outcome of the harnessed energy of a small team of dedicated individuals. It was an accident of history that I happened to be the principal at the time it all started.'

People make organisations; they infuse them with their own passions and enthusiasms. It is *people* that matter in education more than systems or theories when it comes to turning ideas into reality - especially when they need to be made relevant to local communities.

[DS/AS]

References

1   Newman, Michael (1979) *The Poor Cousin - A study of adult education,* George Allen & Unwin

2   Adult Community College, Colchester (2000) *If it wasn't for my class - adult students talk about the value of their learning* Signals Media Arts

3   Learning & Skills Council (2003) *Learning and Skills Council Corporate Plan to 2006 - delivering skills, delivering success*

4   Conner, M.L. *Andragogy and Pedagogy* Ageless Learner 1997-2004. http://agelesslearner.com/intros/andragogy.html

4

Learning Stories of Local People

Adults have complicated lives. Even people who are keen to continue, or return to, education may find that their learning journey is anything but smooth. However, it is clear how important education is when committed lifelong learners describe their experiences.

Pat Goodall

Pat, an active and lively grandmother, is representative of many of the people who have used Grey Friars on and off throughout their professional and social lives. Like many women of her generation who were born around the Second World War, she left school at 15 with no formal qualifications. Her first job, arranged by her mother, was as an office junior in a biscuit factory. It lasted less than a year. Pat soon sought to improve her basic skills and learned shorthand and typing at what was then the Technical College on North Hill.

She got married and had three babies in seven years which prevented her from furthering her education. When the children were at primary and secondary school her interest in *their* education prompted her to think again about her own. By then Grey Friars was established and she enrolled there to take GCE 'O' levels in several subjects. Once the youngest child started senior school, she thought 'It was about time I got a proper job'. She enrolled on a Training Opportunity Scheme in 1977, took a diploma in secretarial skills and worked happily enough for five years in a large business.

The desire for education does not die in some people; it remains beneath the surface and when it is fulfilled it enables someone like Pat, in common with so many people who use Grey Friars, to finally achieve goals that they were prevented from reaching when younger.

She says, 'In September 1982 I went to evening classes at Colchester Institute and achieved an A Level.' With that and her previous certificates she won a place at Essex University and did a history degree. She continues, 'I saw my time at the university as a bit of an indulgence. A goal I never thought I would reach, or would never have the opportunity to aspire to.' She is unduly modest. Until her retirement in 1999 she used her skills to good effect working in various secretarial and administrative posts. In 2000 she returned to Grey Friars and started to catch up with the technical revolution by enrolling on a computer course. She says, 'In 2002 I completed an ECDL (European Computer Driving Licence) which entailed covering seven modules. What a struggle, but it gave me perhaps my greatest sense of achievement!'

Valerie Elliston

The age of a student bears no relationship to how lively they will become during a course. Valerie joined a creative writing class and became one of the students we all want to listen to. Apart from the general interest in her point of view, she had the best grasp of grammar and spelling of all of us (including the tutor). She had been an English tutor herself, but was comparatively inexperienced at writing fiction. She writes:

'I was a tutor in A Level and GCSE Language and Literature at Grey Friars and Colchester Institute during the l980s and l990s. I grew up during the Second World War with parents in perpetual conflict. My father, a branch manager for Elders and Fyffes, the fruit importers, was keen for me to go to Tiffin's Girls' School in Kingston-upon-Thames, then an excellent grammar school, now top of the league tables. However, my mother insisted on a small local convent school similar to the one she herself had attended in a previous generation. I was happy there, but education was almost non-existent: godliness and cleanliness, prayer and panamas were paramount. Luckily, one teacher inspired a lifelong love of English literature, Shakespeare and Chaucer in particular.

My parents finally split up during the War, causing a family upheaval that resulted in my leaving school early without worthwhile qualifications, but with the need to support myself. I began nursing training at St Mary's Hospital, Paddington, but eventually had to exchange this for more lucrative employment as father had by then divorced mother for desertion and there was no maintenance forthcoming for the family, including my younger brother still at school.

I took a clerical job and trained at evening classes in shorthand, typing, book-keeping and commercial French. This has stood me in good stead ever since, especially combined with a knowledge of medical terminology, so that I was eventually able to enjoy working for several years as private secretary to the Director of Surgery at Guy's Hospital, one of the happiest periods of my life. This job would have continued but for the fact that I met and married a Suffolk arable farmer.

I threw myself into the new life which, unfortunately, coincided with a period of very low grain prices. Three children were born during those seven lean years and, eventually, the small farm was sold. I became secretary and researcher to a well-known novelist and screenwriter, discovering a window on the world that was totally different from anything I had previously experienced. The impact of new ideas was astonishing. To cut a long story short, details of the Open University, then only recently established, were casually tossed across the desk to me. That did it. I shall never forget devouring details of the A100 Humanities course which included introductions to art, music, history and literature, above all *Hamlet*. I registered with the OU and, as they say, never looked back. Those enticing Units began to land on the mat and I discovered the delight of writing essays, and endless discussion with other people, especially at the first Summer School where participants ended up knowing one another's deepest thoughts on any topic – but never surnames or backgrounds!

All this was enthusiastically shared by our three children, who were at varying stages between 11 plus and A Levels. We studied together and their support was ever invaluable. Unfortunately, this did not include my husband who, like many others, was in turns bewildered, irritated, and generally felt threatened. However, none of that could stop me, so intense was the compulsion to continue. The degree course took five years, with two courses in the final year. I graduated with a 2.1 and eventually began teaching at Grey Friars and its centres at Stanway School and Sixth Form College, also at Colchester Institute. (By this time, my husband had become permanently disabled owing to a serious car accident, and has been unable to return to work.)

Being able to pass all the hard-won knowledge on to others was the ultimate reward. Each session was like Christmas. Opening a new book on the list was like unwrapping a present for us all. We had fun with the unforgettable *Wife of Bath*; heartache with the rejection of Falstaff; arguments over *The Taming of the Shrew*; suspense with the adventures of *Rogue Male*; endless discussions over the finer points of English grammar and punctuation. Later, I was invited to originate and deliver courses in English usage for publishers and other businesses in London, Cambridge, Oxford and Edinburgh. I also qualified as a professional indexer and still continue this work as a freelance.

In February 2004, I became a student at Grey Friars for the first time, on a creative writing course called Innovations. Setting foot in the main entrance after a long absence, I saw the same glass case exhibiting the latest achievements of students, and the walls festooned with even more notices suggesting, exhorting, encouraging. People smiled in greeting although many were now strangers. The whole place called out, 'Come on! What are you waiting for?'

So I responded, having wanted for years to write fiction, but having succeeded in publishing only non-fiction: a few magazine or journal articles, a number of book reviews for a learned journal, hundreds of book indexes, and a glossary to a still current Spanish course for the BBC.

On the first evening, it felt very strange to be a student, not a tutor. I had to tell myself to lie low for a change! There were about twelve of us by the time the course settled down, almost equally divided between men and women. This resulted in a most interesting mixture of ideas and approaches to the work. One of the men was obviously an old hand; he introduced each of us to the next arrival until the class was complete, producing a welcome to calm the wary waiting moments as we eyed one another and wondered what would happen. We needn't have worried: it was clear from the start that we were actually going to *write*; we weren't going to waffle around. Our tutor announced our aims and objectives for the course and off we went.

Writing is a solitary, perhaps lonely, pursuit, so it was a delight to feel that our efforts were going to be read and discussed by others. However, this was also a risk, exposing our failings to strangers, to such an extent that we were at first reluctant to give honest responses, fearing to hurt feelings and knowing only too well that our own turns would come. A contribution would be read out and greeted with initial silence as we wondered just how to react. Our tutor pointed out this pitfall at the start and set the example of her own professional criticism delivered with common sense and tact. She gave us tips and handouts to guide us on our way so that, as time went on, we relaxed and our responses accordingly became more worthwhile as we learned the techniques of writing and had more to say on the subject. The variety of pieces produced was surprising, from the most evocative accounts of travel in exotic places to sensitively observed descriptions of human interaction - sometimes humorous - not to mention a few adventures in other worlds.

My own experience of non-fiction writing was quite a handicap as, in the midst of a piece of fiction, up would pop my urge to treat the readers to a fascinating piece of history or geography. 'No!' cried our long-suffering tutor, 'that won't do!' so on I went, excising my favourite sections, trying to show without telling - that perennial bugbear of the creative writing student. However, there were others for whom this was far less of a problem, so we were able to learn from one another in the way adult students do so well.

Interaction among the students was most interesting: we began as strangers, but gradually formed a common bond, often encouraging one another. In some cases, pieces were exchanged by email, and responses eagerly sought. By the end of the course, we really felt we had learned more about our own writing and were inspired to continue.

Yes, that's the word, *inspiration*, that sums up the Grey Friars spirit.'

We are often struck by the 'Grey Friars' effect, that almost indescribable something that affects students, tutors and others who work here. It becomes clearer when you speak to past tutors and students.

Many tutors speak with such warmth of their experiences. There can be many reasons. Adult motivations can be strong and varied and when enthusiasm is common to teacher and learners, the whole experience is enhanced for everybody. Adult students have a tremendous range of backgrounds and they bring a wealth of experiences to class, which enriches the learning environment. There can be a quality of interaction between students and tutors which is variously stimulating, challenging, enlightening and egalitarian.

Great pleasure can be taken in observing the progress of students - with some achieving the previously unthinkable transition from 'basic skills' classes to further and higher education. A sense of value and worth can be felt by all who work in such an environment.

A good example has always been given by senior staff at Grey Friars. Management over the decades has been flexible, focused, strategic and caring towards staff and students. As a result, a general ethos of helpfulness has been evident over the years and this includes the support staff, many of whom are willing to go several steps further than might have been required.

Many people take genuine delight and pleasure from working in a historical building which still retains many original features and suggestions of a bygone age; the pleasant space it occupies; its proximity to the park and established, residential streets - right in the centre of town.

Roger Moores

Roger is the sort of person of whom another student once said, 'That chap, I can't remember his name - the one who makes everyone in the group feel at ease.' He has this to say about his experience of Grey Friars:

'I first went to Grey Friars eleven years ago when I needed to learn Windows, so I knew something about the place. Five years later I retired. There's nothing like retirement. You can flop all day in front of the box, watching sharks, crocodiles, Napoleon and Hitler. It's great, for a time. But the same programmes tend to come round again - and again - so you have to *do* something.

So now I go to learn many things, but mainly to get my regular fix of Creative Writing, in the hope of one day writing that better-than-average book, and I'm getting better all the time. Other people, who come in all shapes and ages, may go for different reasons: to get qualified, to improve skills, to learn art, history, to do crafts, to learn fitness techniques, social skills.

If you go by car, watch out for the understandable, but sadistic rules about car park closure. Your car could get locked in at night. For evening sessions, I go by bus. I get there early; my shoes squeak on the tessellated floor (though I've paid for them) and I go though the back door, and treat myself to a refreshing pint (one only - I assure you, have the rest after class) at the Forester's before class starts.

Experts may say that Grey Friars is not fit for its purpose and - unlike today's grey, glass walled, exam-factories - it is old, rambling, and creaky. It needs a lift (one that goes up and down I mean - please subscribe to the fund). Though it was once a school and is now a college, it is just a comfortable, friendly old town house. You are welcome. There's an atmosphere. It's not just the building. It's the people, who are friendly and helpful.

Unlike my memory of school, there's no hierarchy that shows; you meet people at all academic levels, and of all ages – not just ancient adolescents like me – and at the coffee breaks you can talk to them. The little coffee bar sells my family firm's biscuits, all the way from Dorset.

Four things happen. You learn things – for qualifications, for skill-enhancement, or just for the sake of learning them. You want to learn more things. Creative writing leads to literature, art, history and languages. You make new friends.

It's enjoyable. It's a risk free setting.

I'd been a writer of sorts: management books, and a bit of industrial journalism. But none of that can be described as creative – so I've come back to Grey Friars mainly, but not exclusively, to become a creative writer. And I think I'm nearly there.

It's professional. Our tutors are top class. We have to set objectives at the beginning of each course. It's a good idea if you can set these goals and targets down in behavioural terms – which means things you'll be able to do after the course that you couldn't do before. But don't let learning objectives destroy the magic. You may wish to keep it a secret; if you're like me, you've really come to learn, as George Mallory said, *because it's there.*

So, go on. Push open that front door, and get something back for the taxes you paid all those years. If you love art, folly, or the bright eyes of students, speed to Grey Friars.'

Sally Petts

Sally is another committed lifelong learner. She writes:

'My connection with Grey Friars goes back a long way, about 20 years, to my first abortive attempts at throwing a pot in pottery class, just after I moved to the area. My pots always fell off the wheel, so I stuck to making clay sculpture. I thought typing skills might be useful, so my cousin and I learned to type.

My long-term interest in painting was reawakened, after child number two, when I attended a brilliant summer school in 1987 with Dione Page who taught flower painting. Several flower paintings later, and the birth of child number three, I went to some short evening courses in drawing and watercolours. I suddenly realised I was quite good at painting – my appetite was whetted. I needed and wanted more. With my youngest settled safely in the crèche I embarked on the Art Link course with an eye to further education. I gained the portfolio I needed and confidence to continue. David, my son, was fascinated by Reg, the caretaker, who visited the crèche every week. Some of David's first words were "Where's Reg?" This question continued even when I had moved on to the Colchester Institute to continue my art education (we did visit occasionally). After a two-year course at the institute, I attended Suffolk College, and in 1996 attained a degree in Art and Design. I had fulfilled my childhood dream to become an artist.

Even during my further education I had not abandoned Grey Friars because I needed to practise life drawing. By then I had moved to Mersea, so I went to Don Butlin's life drawing class. Following graduation I felt I needed to keep fit, so I joined a yoga class.

I decided I would like to teach art to adults (a complete change of career - I was formerly a scientist, working in research laboratories). So back to Grey Friars, for my first job teaching, a short art course at Brightlingsea in 1997. I needed teacher training qualifications, most of which I studied at Grey Friars. I now teach eight varied art classes a week.

I have just finished a short course in Salsa dancing with my son (now aged 20) and his girlfriend because we had all watched "Strictly Ballroom"!

Being involved with Grey Friars has literally changed my life. It enabled me to fulfil my dreams and ambitions, to paint and teach. I am lucky enough to do a job I love. While I continue to develop as an artist, my students come on the journey of discovery with me. When I try new techniques in painting, so do they. It's a two way process, because I often get new ideas from my students.

I am passionate about art, there needs to be as much of it as possible, available for everyone who wishes to try something creative. We all need to tap into our creativity. A true community college like Grey Friars gives everyone that opportunity. It may be we cannot fulfil our dreams until retirement, when the need for paper qualifications has passed. We can still learn and develop new skills, interests and friends. Funding for a college like Grey Friars should never be in question rather we should be asked how much money we need to bring more people into contact with the wealth of opportunities available within it.

I hope that it will still be here when I retire. I still need to learn ballroom dancing (may do that next year!). I want to be able to throw that pot in pottery, I fancy trying sculpture and stained glass window making, and I never got over failing my O Level French – but it's not too late!'

Sally ended her description with a list of her qualifications: BA (Hons) Art and Design, Cert.Ed., PGCE, RSA Stage 1 Typing – 'All because of Grey Friars!'

Marion Walls

Many people have used Grey Friars as an addition to an already full life, but what the institution has offered Marion has been a far more profound life changing experience. Marion's story shows what can be achieved by someone determined to succeed in climbing the academic ladder. She has become one of the high achievers of Colchester's adult education system.

Marion was born in the West Country and came from a family that didn't have high expectations for a girl's education. Rather the opposite in fact. Her Mum who worked as a cleaner didn't share any of Marion's ambitions and didn't want her to go to grammar school, although she passed the 11+ exam. 'I always felt I didn't fit. I wasn't allowed to play with the other children on the estate.'

Her father, himself an early school leaver, did however attend 'night school' and WEA and eventually became an accountant. What both parents considered suitable and safe for their daughter was a job as a bank clerk when she left school at 16. 'At that time it was considered a good job for a girl.'

Marion believes her choices were limited by the parental attitude of 'Why educate a girl? She is only going to get married.' Marion married a soldier while still in her teens and had children. As an army wife she was posted to Germany where she did some voluntary and then paid work in primary schools and worked with emotionally deprived children. 'I've always been a working mother.' In Germany she had a thirst for learning and took part in many workshops and training classes, qualifying as a teaching assistant. The family stayed 22 years in Germany. She would have preferred to return sooner, but keeps a positive view of their life there.

Marion went back to education via evening classes at Grey Friars. The couple grew apart and the marriage finally ended when Marion developed cancer in her forties. She overcame this life threatening illness. Her son and daughter are now in their 20s and a younger boy is still at school.

In spite of her life-threatening cancer Marion was driven to continue studying. Whilst in bed for the best part of a year, she began a re-evaluation of her life and decided to do what she had always wanted to do – to write and to study. Although, at one point she was given five weeks to live, she agreed to take a new treatment which has succeeded in containing her cancer and, although not cured, Marion continues to live a full life.

Her older children had already left home when she started to study again. Her youngest child was used to Mum doing homework as well as him. At Grey Friars she studied for A-levels under Mrs Madge and others who inspired her. 'If you're an adult, the pressure is off.' She was studying without the support of her partner.

In 2000 Marion achieved a BA with 2.1 honours in Literature and Sociology from Essex University. The following year she achieved a distinction in her MA from the same university.

Being a single parent, in spite of the hardships this entails, has helped her academic aspirations. 'Some men can become insecure if their wives become more highly educated.'

Marion had rarely visited a theatre, but had read all her life. 'I always wrote poetry and music and was published as a teenager, through a local church.'

Marion is now well into her PhD at Essex University. Perhaps because of her background, her interests are particularly focused on class and education studies. She finds it a financial struggle. She has to pay her own fees for the first three years. She finds it "rather ironic" that her ex-husband's maintenance fees will pay part of her learning fees. To help finance her PhD, Marion teaches an undergraduate course on "The Enlightenment".

Marion's experience of Grey Friars has been completely positive. She found the building and its historic character user-friendly. 'People who teach only adults, like Mrs Madge, were brilliant.'

'I quite often read a book to inspire myself - someone like Simone de Beauvoir or Lorna Sage.' After the PhD she intends to continue teaching and to write articles for the academic press.

Grey Friars has an influence beyond its walls. Current principal Alan Skinner told about what he describes as his 'best few months in the profession for many years' when he 'returned to the roots of adult education as a result of working with residents of the Greenstead estate'.

Winston Browne

Alan Skinner first met Winston when Ted Crunden, then a County Councillor, came to Grey Friars to discuss adult learning opportunities on the Greenstead estate. Winston had contacted Ted because he wished to see the local people take an active part in determining opportunities for their self-development, training and learning. There had been a number of further education and training projects introduced in the area over the years, but they had all eventually either come to an end or faded away.

He painted a picture of local people as the passive recipients of a diet of opportunities served up by outsiders who arrived, operated for a short while and then disappeared, leaving a void. Winston had moved to Colchester from London and was aware of the kind of short-term, high profile, but short-lived activities that could be made available. He was sure that was not what Greenstead needed. Alan remembers him saying quite clearly, 'We need something local, something we can rely on. I am willing to give time to help you get to know the people and ask them what they need.'

The story of the College's involvement which followed this meeting is told in Chapter 10. Alan, however, is convinced that without Winston's involvement, there would not have been such a significant and positive outcome.

'Winston's help, encouragement and example was just what I needed at the time to reaffirm my belief in the relevance of a community education approach. After 1992, Adult Education had been drawn in to chasing funding and meeting targets and as a result had become insular. Winston's offer to broker interaction with people who live on the Greenstead estate came as a breath of fresh air. I readily accepted his help and decided I would personally represent the College and take to the streets. Forget the meetings and emails for a while – I was off to discuss education with local people!'

Jahanara Loqueman

Jahanara has been a driving force in bringing a wide range of Asian women into contact with Grey Friars especially through outreach and family learning activities.

A soft-spoken woman in her early sixties, she wears traditional dress and keeps her hair covered in a white scarf. Jahanara was born in Sylhet, then a part of Pakistan. She finished primary education and then went to a girls' college where she completed two years of a degree course but, she says with a wry laugh, marriage intervened. However it was comparatively rare in those days to have got as far as she did and she could not have done so without her father's support. Her family was fairly progressive in those days with regard to women's education. Her father, a studious man, was unable to complete university studies because he had to help support his younger brothers, both of whom were able to go to university. Grandmother didn't consider girls should have higher education, but her uncle said, 'If girls are not educated they won't get a good husband.' Jahanara's early years were spent in an extended South Asian family.

So the culture shock when her new husband brought her to the UK was considerable. Although she had studied English she could not understand the rapidity of native English speakers and she found the mixing of men and women unnerving. When her husband used to bring his friends home to taste pakoras and other delicacies, she was too shy to speak and unable to go out alone. This social isolation is common among South Asian women transferred to a country with a cold climate and customs they neither approve nor understand. Jahanara was unusual in the way she gradually overcame the barriers and has become what she is now, a leader and a spokesperson for her community and for their unmet needs.

Of her early years in Colchester she says simply, 'I was like a fish out of the sea.' Colloquial English foxed her and she used to hide in the toilet to avoid having to speak to people. With the help of her husband, this gradually changed. Jahanara made friends with two English women, took English lessons and slowly began to adjust to British life. In the late sixties her daughters were born and taking them to the park meant that she had to go outdoors herself.

When she arrived she did not know any other Bengali-speaking women in Colchester. The few other South Asians spoke Urdu and Gujerati. In the course of time Jahanara has learned Urdu and after forty years residence her English is fluent. Her husband ran a restaurant for twenty years and she found herself having to help out when staffing was short. 'I had to talk to the customers,' she said. 'At first I was terribly shy about speaking English.' In 1987 the Loquemans sold the restaurants and Jahanara's involvement came to an end. Their four children were either at college or secondary school. Jahanara found that as with many housewives who have brought up a family and possibly run a business, her skills were not seen as transferable. At the Job Centre there were few opportunities for her. However, she had already begun the voluntary work and community work for which she is now so well known.

She came to Grey Friars to do a six weeks Work Preparation course. She says now that the course helped her learn how to present herself and gave added self confidence but getting a job was still a frustrating experience. She knew she wanted to work in the field of health but did not have enough qualifications. Although she failed the entrance examination, she was still accepted to start nurse training. The Nursing Director interviewed her and said, 'I think that you will make a wonderful nurse.' She has always regretted that a weak back meant that she was unable to complete the course. She was not strong enough for the physical effort needed. She took a factory job making tiny parts for one year and then decided that she could not continue working just with her fingers, she needed to use her mind.

She found the right niche for herself not locally but in Tower Hamlets which has a large Bengali community. Jahanara worked on various projects. She found many problems in the community that were not being addressed by the social and health services. Of concern were problems relating to incontinence amongst both old and young males as well as females. Although incontinence is also found among the white community, making help available was complicated by the language and social barriers. Jahanara ran a project called National Asian Continence Promotion and Training. The project was successful and innovative. Jahanara received two European awards and was asked to speak at international conferences. She still continues this work. She is proud of these awards; in 1997 the Commonwealth Award for Excellence and Good Practice in Women's Health and the following year as the only British winner of the first European Health Education Award for the United Kingdom.

In the last few years she has become involved in Grey Friars again; no longer as a student but as an informal advisor between the Bangladeshi community in the town and the services provided by the establishment. Was it chance or destiny that led her to this role? She picked up a leaflet in the library inviting those concerned to a meeting about a Primary Health Trust and decided to go along. By this time many more Bangladeshi women had arrived in Colchester. The overwhelming majority had come to be with their husbands and only a tiny minority were educated in a Western style or spoke good English. Jahanara discerned a lack of interest among the Bangladeshi community and decided in her forthright manner that she would do something about it. She developed a group for women which is called Bangladeshi Mohila Somity and was given a room by Colchester Voluntary Services to use as a meeting place. From this group, Jahanara encouraged as many of the women as possible to participate in ESOL courses.

Physical activity is generally absent from the lives of many Bangladeshi women. Although many swimming courses are offered by Grey Friars, they are not able to take part. For such women a swimming course has to be taught by another woman and has to be off limits to men. Jahanara in collaboration with Grey Friars staff member Carolyn Roberts arranged with colleagues to run a swimming course adapted to the sensitivities of Asian women. She feels passionately that raising awareness of one ethnic group could and should encourage Grey Friars to attract many more non-native speakers. She saw the enthusiasm engendered in senior tutors such as Joan Wheatley and Chris Hubbard in the Health and Fitness department when they supported new ventures. She wants to see the kind of pioneering work that she has done for the women replicated for Bangladeshi men.

Jahanara's only complaint about Grey Friars is that for so long she didn't know it was there. 'There are amazing activities going on, but it is hard sometimes to find out about them.' She says that the work of the Skills for Life department can bring so many more non-native speakers and asylum seekers into the mainstream. For the moment, however, she sees herself working both paid and voluntarily for the women of her community

[DS]

5

Staff

The people who staff adult education services come from a wide range of backgrounds and carry out a similarly wide range of duties. As recently as the 1980s the majority of adult education centres were staffed by a small number of workers and usually it was only the principal who would have a full-time contract. Everybody would need to assist in administrative and publicity activities and this has undoubtedly resulted in a history of recruitment of people with multiple skills.

Tutors have often come to teach adults by a variety of routes. One of the most obvious sources of staff would, of course, be the schools sector. In chapter 3, Allin Coleman describes the transformation of school teachers to adult educators. The first three tutor stories both reflect and enhance the previous discussion.

Mary Brunning

Mary looks back on her years as a tutor with great pleasure. She had a long and varied career in education. After she married in the 1950s she came to Colchester and taught English for twenty years in various schools, a busy schedule with two young children as well: then came a decade as careers officer for the County Council. Her last years in teaching were spent as a part time tutor in English at Grey Friars

She says, 'Far too often people carry an erroneous label given to them by teachers early in life and it remains with them. But those of us who have taught at Grey Friars know the joy of seeing students gain confidence, develop hitherto unknown skills and thus make huge progress.

For ten years I taught English GCSE Language and Literature classes for which there were supposed to be twelve students to make the course officially viable.' Mary recounts the following incident. 'On the second week when only ten students had arrived and I myself was fearful that the class might have to close. Alan (the principal) came into the room. He quietly assessed the already bonding, working group and cheerfully declared, "I'm not closing this." Great relief all round.'

Mary can give instances where the flexibility of a Grey Friars course benefits the students. She recalls one young woman who was studying both language and literature and who was having appalling problems at home. In tears, the girl said she couldn't continue. Mary advised her to drop out for a time and when or if she returned she would get the help she needed. The girl returned two months later, made up the work she had missed and gained two A grades.

Mary Brunning like so many of the staff at Grey Friars recognizes the real caring that goes on. She says, 'In April 1990 my husband and I were in a road accident. He was killed outright and I suffered severe concussion. By September my doctor was advising me to return to my classes at Grey Friars if I possibly could. When I told Diana McLeod the vice principal, she said that if I got to the door and couldn't face it - she would take over. With this enormous support behind me, prepared but highly nervous, I went into the class. The friendliness of the class took over and I was back again.'

Mary also points out how important the personal care tutors give their students can be. She says, 'Adults of all ages are often nervous about studying again. They can have worries about fees, grants and travel and many other matters. IT can be particularly difficult if they need a certificate at the end of it. I used to encourage them to attend regularly, if possible complete their homework, come to me with any problems and not worry too much about the grade. They would then most likely carry off a certificate.'

Mary, now fully retired, goes to a play-reading once a fortnight at the college. She remembers how warm and friendly the front office staff always were.

'They were indeed ten good years at Grey Friars.'

Present day tutors may grumble at the increase of paperwork, but the loyalty and affection for the institution remains firm. Grey Friars is rightfully proud of the quality of its tutors and the independence of their views. It has always been a part of the Grey Friars managerial approach to set the parameters, make clear the professional requirements and encourage creative expression within these bounds. Past and present staff are keen to assert that the non-formal Grey Friars system, delegating and sharing decision-making and responsibility, does not compromise educational standards. Indeed, quality levels throughout the College's work can be enhanced by all involved feeling a sense of collective ownership.

Claire Hawkins

Claire, teaching English at GCSE level, exemplifies the many dedicated women (and some men) who take on the role of guiding adults through the examination system. These are people who do rather than talk. They will teach adults with a dedication that bears no relation to the modest salaries that they earn. Teaching, like nursing, still retains a vestige of the vocation that the caring professions need. There are over 350 part time tutors.

Claire has been teaching this course for the last five years, but she has been involved with Adult Education for at least twenty.

About 15 years ago, when she first arrived in Essex, she became involved with Access courses at the Colchester Institute. This was when all further and adult education was under the control of Essex County Council. Access courses, designed for adults who want to get back into formal education, form an integral part of Adult Education. For Claire, who believes that education should be lifelong, teaching Access courses meant she could help people who maybe had left school without qualifications get back into the mainstream. They were students often able to progress to higher education - degree courses and professional training such as teaching, nursing and social work.

There are many examples of people whose progress through the system illustrates the importance of the full range of adult education provision. For example one woman who started on a holiday Spanish course at Grey Friars discovered a talent for languages, progressed to an Access course and is now a languages teacher. Another example, a young man in his twenties, written off at school, started a Basic Skills class, was discovered to be dyslexic and via an Access course has now gained a degree in history.

Claire came into adult education by a familiar route. She started out as a secondary school teacher teaching in a variety of schools in various parts of England. She ended up in Sheffield.

'I became pregnant, took time off to have my daughter and then started part time and I did an MA in Continuing Education in Sheffield. That MA course is still going strong.' After that she picked up part time work at Sheffield City Polytechnic in Access courses. Going into further education was more compatible with having small children. She laughs and says that working for Sheffield City Council was very good in those days when David Blunkett was a key figure on the Sheffield City Council in the heady left-wing days when it was laughingly called 'The People's Republic of Sheffield'.

For Claire 'left wing' is a compliment, not pejorative. Not coming from an underprivileged background, she nevertheless has a strong commitment to the idea of education as a part of social justice. Her father, the first of his family to go to university, became a professor. She herself is married to a university professor, is a teacher and speculates whether one of her two daughters may enter the teaching profession after she finishes her degree, making it the third generation to be involved in education.

She had some worries about relocating 'into the Tory heartland at Essex' but establishing her family in Wivenhoe she soon found her fears were unnecessary.

Claire is critical of the directive national environment that teachers have to work in now. 'Grey Friars is actually a humane place,' she says, contrasting its person-centred approaches to the audit culture generated by the present funding and control systems of national and local government. How does she view these national trends in education?

She relates it to government policy. It relates to the need for an educated and qualified workforce and ways chosen to achieve this, which may not necessarily reach those who most need support. The funding now tends to be given to specific high-profile projects rather than supporting a community-based system open to everybody. Claire remarks that there is great deal of rhetoric about the need for lifelong learning in its widest sense, but 'there's no money put into it.' The current emphasis in post-16 education on skills for employment creates a narrow instrumental definition of education and ignores the enormous influence that it can have on improving the quality of people's lives at all stages. Claire like so many of the staff at Grey Friars believes that the value of education throughout life should be recognized and receive state support ('money, not just rhetoric!').

This would require that the state embrace a wider definition of education to include all the life-enhancing aspects, which far from being luxuries are vital to individuals. People who participate in education are more likely to be fit and healthy and contribute actively to community life as well as the economy. This is being well documented by research undertaken by the Wider Benefits of Learning projects at Birkbeck College and the University of London Institute of Education. Claire is referring to all the non-accredited subjects that have to prove their 'worth' in a competitive environment.

'It's all those skills that cannot be measured that contribute to a person's sense of well-being.' Claire argues, as so many of us in Adult Education are doing, about the worth of so-called 'recreational' courses. 'What really annoys me,' says Claire 'is the attitude that you can make a clear distinction between vocational and non-vocational education. It isn't as simple as saying people need structured vocational learning for a particular qualification for a job. Of course it is important to provide good, structured vocational skills training which prepares people for jobs. But it isn't that simple. There are those people who may step into an adult education college and try painting or creative writing. They can discover things about themselves that they didn't know before. To become confident, more articulate and feel good about yourself would mean you would make a better employee anyway. You can't measure that.'

Claire remarks that even in a course like her own, GCSE English, various issues come up. Students come with very different educational backgrounds and aspirations and guidance often becomes an integral part of working with individuals.

For Claire, the non-accredited courses are valuable not simply for themselves, but also as a means of promoting self-worth. 'They start people off on learning,' she says. 'For example, someone might start out on a decoupage course and then go on to do some further maths.'

Claire doesn't think much of the 'learning styles' questionnaires that tutors are supposed to give to all their students, but she can sympathise with management who have to be 'loyal to their employers' and support these sorts of initiatives. She thinks, however, that such initiatives will eventually die a natural death.

The obsession with measuring quality, value for money and efficiency, arising from the business and commercial ethic invading education, has reduced much assessment of learning to the completion of forms and tick boxes. 'This wastes the time and energy of both tutors and students, interferes with classroom activities and doesn't result in a better experience for students. ILPs (Individual Learning Plans) stem from laudable aims, namely to provide constructive and regular feedback to students of their work and how it is progressing, but as they are constituted at present, ILPs are invasive, unwieldy and often filled in so speedily as to be worthless.' Claire's solution is to adapt ILPs to 'make them more relevant to the course. I ignore the instruction that they should be completed after every session, and only use them as a supplement to the other, more valuable forms of communication with students.'

Claire like many tutors condemns the widening use of the all-in-one form. She says, 'The universal application of simplistic learning styles questionnaires is a pointless activity and an example of the need to provide 'pieces of paper evidence' of a college's 'student-centred' approach, without any critical examination of their value and effects.'

At the start of a GCSE course Claire will have twenty students. Because they are adults with complicated lives, a number will probably drop out. Claire sees her work as helping people who may start from a very low base in terms of knowledge and confidence. 'I get them to a level where they can progress. It's labour intensive, but that is what I bought into.' She smiles to imply that that is the real reward – when her students make progress. She is not teaching for the monetary rewards. 'The pay is barely at the level of the minimum wage, once the time spent in preparing the classes and marking student work is considered.'

Claire is one of many who believe that the atmosphere of Grey Friars, and the building itself, is a great help in promoting that feeling of confidence in the students. A colleague who agrees with this is Peter Bailey, who was once the Chairman of the Members' Association and worked hard to maintain not only the inclusive nature of Grey Friars life, but also to ensure that the building was preserved as a base for local adult education.

Peter Bailey

Peter told us: 'I'm not an Essex boy. I came from Hampshire.' Peter did a degree in Sociology at London University and then took up a teaching career, the bulk of which has been spent at the same school in Tiptree. He married

Wendy in 1976. Having a degree didn't necessarily give him a professional job that he liked so he worked happily on a building site. He was astonished one day to find that several of his fellow workers didn't know how to read an advertisement hoarding. He had not met adult illiteracy before. He read them the notice and thought that he might like to teach adults to read.

'We were quite poor. I eventually went back to college to do a post-graduate Certificate in Education.' Peter went on to teach Business Studies in the secondary school sector.

In his secondary school in Tiptree, used as an outstation for Grey Friars, he got to know some of the evening tutors. Both for the sake of teaching adults and for the extra cash he took on teaching a course about money in the modern world. His course was a great success and he was offered Sociology GCE O Level at Tiptree and for ten years he never looked back. He found himself after a year teaching GCE A Level and O Level at Grey Friars itself in the early eighties, although he continued with his day job at the secondary school.

'Teaching sixth-formers was fine but teaching adults was altogether a new experience for me – teaching disaffected women wanting to get back into the groove and quite a lot of non-commissioned officers on their way out of the Army, paid by the MOD to study as a way of getting back into civilian life.' Peter found that group of students amazingly proficient and reliable over assignments - any time you spoke to them they stood to attention and said 'yessir'. Also, the generally curious, school drop-outs, an eclectic group of people. 'I thoroughly enjoyed that and the subject matter. We got quite good exam results.'

'I ended up teaching three nights a week as well as daytime in school. I toddled off on my bike.' He taught the A Level at the Sixth Form College but always preferred teaching at Grey Friars. He loved the atmosphere there. Something we hear repeated over and over again.

Peter continued teaching O Level after he stopped A Level when Wendy returned to work and he needed to be at home for the children after school. He left tutoring when he took a secondment to work at the BBC. He didn't go back to Grey Friars, but the memories remain warm.

Some people have come to adult education as a second career in education. Although this is the case with our next interviewee, he is also one of those tutors who breaks any preconceptions you might have of the sort of person who teaches adults.

Bill Tamblyn

Whereas some female tutors have come into Adult Education after leaving teaching to have babies, it is more usual for some of the male tutors to enter the sector after other careers. One such is Professor Bill Tamblyn, the recently retired director of Colchester Institute's department of music, which he headed for twenty years. Bill is currently running the Quire, a music group at the college's Wilson Marriage Centre and he has plans for many other courses. He has a passionate commitment to adult education in its wider and broader definitions of lifelong learning.

Now in his early sixties, he considers that he's led something of a charmed life. His parents were not well-off and lived in rented rooms in Birmingham, but young William won a scholarship to the grammar school in the early 1950s. Unequivocally he says, 'They were the happiest days of my life.' Music came early. The grammar school music master asked Bill to join a church choir where he was choirmaster. It was the Aston Church choir, already well-known for broadcasts and concerts and of a national standard. Although the Tamblyns were notionally Methodists, his Mum had no objections to him singing in an Anglican choir. Bill's career has always been helped by interventions. He dismisses them as lucky, but I'd think his talent and personality have prompted all those helping hands.

When Bill was twelve, his choirmaster sent him to a piano teacher. The family could not have afforded the fees, but the teacher guaranteed to give Bill a scholarship and to teach him until he went to college. Although he remarks ruefully 'she never taught me to sight-read music,' he achieved a Grade V111 in piano (the highest exam qualification). He was also a young composer and won the Open Competition in the Birmingham Music Festival on three occasions. Bill hadn't thought of entering - it was his music teacher who sent off the winning piece.

At Durham, where he read music, he idolized the Professor of Music, Arthur Hutching. Years later over a pub lunch it transpired that the head of music had been born and brought up in the same village as Bill's father. 'Hutching was extremely kind to me,' says Bill, 'giving me his review copies of records because he knew I could not afford to buy my own.'

Bill played these records on a portable record player that had mysteriously arrived on his doorstep one Christmas when he was twelve years old. Who gave it to him?

The mystery was solved while Bill was at university and had an operation on his hand. The young surgeon who operated told him that his father, a local Birmingham GP, had found out how much Bill loved music and knowing how hard-up the family was, had bought and given the young musician a record player anonymously.

'With that kind of start in life, you cannot go wrong,' Bill says. He evinces no apparent regret that he has not gone on to become a famous composer or an international pianist, 'But what I have done in the last forty years is to try to pass on the exuberance that music brings.'

He has seen his career as a type of mission. 'I have devoted my energy to give back to other people what I've received.' He says, 'I am a teacher. I teach music and what it can give to so many other people.'

The major part of his teaching career has been as head of music at Colchester Institute. Even then he says he was conscious of the needs of the mature student. 'Among maybe 200 students for our music degree, I would have around forty mature students.' At that time that was a high proportion. One graduate was seventy. Mature students who come into music may do so either to try a change of career or simply to understand something that they have loved. Amongst mature students who have studied under Bill at the Institute he numbers ex-Army people or adults leaving business activities.

Bill left Colchester Institute when he was sixty-two. He had been in full time teaching for forty years and wanted a change. An active man, he sees another twenty years ahead of him in this new career of bringing music to adults on a part time basis. His work at the Institute was a good preparation.

'Over the past five years, I've become increasingly concerned with the ineptitude of successive governments in dealing with the aspirations of those who want to pursue music to understand music, not just play the notes. To that end, he is hoping that he can extend the music classes at Grey Friars to include music appreciation. 'All I want of my mature students,' says Bill, 'is an open mind. You don't get the same response with a group of 16 year-olds as you do with a group of over 50s.'

On the importance of Adult Education for the active elderly, he is adamant. 'These are people who have paid their taxes throughout their working lives. Now they have a right to publicly-supported adult education.'

Bill believes that music studies of all sorts are one of the best ways to foster community and shared experience. He points out that the mature singer won't have a voice of star quality, but will have a lifetime's experience to put into their singing. He illustrates this with an anecdote of teaching on his summer school a revolutionary South African women's song. They were white, mainly middle-aged, middle class women, but they were able to enter the mindset of their South African sisters living under apartheid.

Music for mature students is not a form of therapy, Bill insists. It is connecting with the real world through the medium of sound. He says of the modern television culture, 'We are dominated by the visual image.'

Does Bill think there is a future for his part time music courses in current adult education? He is aware that there are government pressures to siphon money away from non-accredited courses. He says he has a missionary zeal to promote music now. 'If the money isn't forthcoming, we will have to raise it ourselves,' he says.

A constantly recurring theme when one discusses classes with students is how much more many tutors bring to the class beyond the subject matter of the course. The variety of tutors at Grey Friars is astonishing; often their only similarity is the commitment they bring to adult education. A typical tutor who is as untypical as you could ever find is Larissa, the specialist in Russian language and culture.

Larissa Wymer

Larissa teaches Russian at Grey Friars both GCE A Level and GCSE. She is a large and beautiful native Russian in her early fifties, who in spite of speaking fluent English has kept her Russian accent. She embodies the quality and diversity of the tutors we met.

Her father, himself a Party member, had fallen out of favour and was sent into exile in a small town outside Novgorod. She grew up as a young communist in spite of the sad fact that exile broke her father's heart and he died when she was seven. 'I went through all the stages a communist child goes through. I was a complete believer. Communist ideas seemed to me like Christian ideas.' Larissa's mother was Jewish and Larissa experienced anti-Semitism as a school child. That was the downside. The upside was her mother's encouragement and belief in her. In spite of poverty Larissa had a university education. 'My generation did become highly educated.'

Larissa studied Chemistry at Leningrad (now St Petersburg). But her early career in Russia was in theatre administration. This ties in with her love, and immense knowledge, of Russian literature and culture - qualities that she brings to her language teaching so that her courses are not just language-based but are also a lesson in Russian culture.

In Leningrad she met an English engineer, one of the first who was seconded to Russia, married him and came to Britain in 1985, but this marriage ended in divorce. Some years later Larissa met a teacher and has been happily married ever since. Her husband teaches in Norwich where they still have their home and Larissa began to teach Russian.

Since 1990 she has been teaching Russian at the University of Essex. She showed me the text book she has written, which is published by the university. The Russian department at Essex like that of University of East Anglia in Norwich has closed down so Larissa now teaches Russian not at degree level but rather A Level standard. 'There are a number of reasons for the decline of interest in the Russian language, one of them is the decline of teaching Russian in comprehensive schools and there is a fear of the difficulty.' Larissa would like Russian language to gain more popularity. 'In the world at least two hundred million people speak Russian,' she says. She has travelled widely in the old Soviet Union and is well read in Russian literature. She has always wanted to share this knowledge and that has been one of the principal motivations for her to become involved with adult education.

'I was very brave,' she says. 'I was living in Norwich and I offered to lecture on Russian Civilisation in my poor English. I think they accepted because it was a novelty. There were no Soviet women living in Norwich offering courses. It was fun for me and fun for the audience. We developed an atmosphere of incredible friendship. The audience would correct my English.' The success of these lectures led Larissa to offer to teach Russian at the equivalent of Grey Friars in Norwich.

In the early nineties Larissa was teaching at Essex, when one of her colleagues who taught Russian at Grey Friars dropped out, and Larissa stepped in to plug the gap. Her courses have been incredibly successful. Nowadays she teaches three GCSE courses. The examination results are excellent. Of eight A Level students sitting the exam in 2004, seven achieved an A and one a B.

'The Russian language is terribly hard,' says Larissa. 'I was tremendously proud of them.' Her students come from various social backgrounds. 'All kinds of people come to classes, their ages range from the early thirties to sixty-five, one is a lorry driver, and another is a nun.' Larissa finds that she has as many men as women in her groups.

Last Easter she took ten students to Russia. They made friends in Russia and invited them to come and stay in England. The students raised the money themselves for the trips. These study trips are a great feature of the language and art departments. Trips to Italy and France are often arranged, as well as to other locations worldwide.

Larissa expresses distaste for the increase in bureaucracy. 'I think it undermines the trust in the tutor that when I first came here existed between the administration and the teachers. Exam results show if we are effective professionals. If results are good, it is mutual achievement by the students and by the tutor.' Larissa explains, 'In adult education, you have people of all social backgrounds, people of different age groups plus people who come from university or others who can hardly spell.' It is widely acknowledged that it is enormously hard for the tutor to accommodate such a wide range within a scheme of work written before a class has enrolled. 'That is where schemes of work can become a fiction because although it is wonderful to write a scheme, nobody can follow it without making dramatic changes. Something simple could happen, someone may miss a lesson you have to go back or some understand quicker than others. During the lessons the unexpected can happen.'

Filling in forms: Larissa shrugs her shoulders, raises her eyes to heaven and clearly shows she thinks much of this is a waste of teaching time. She says. 'Forms do not prove our determination or achievement.' Does she consider that this strong view is held by many teachers of adult education?

'Paperwork destroys the confidence of the teacher. Last academic year I had an inspection. The inspector didn't speak Russian herself. She was watching how I gave my class. Once the lesson finished she said that she was very glad to see such a good atmosphere. Then she asked for the paperwork, I said the wrong thing. I said I did not have any. I only had a teaching material file - very full. I prepare that before every class. So the assessment said my lesson was a very good level and my students were happy, but I did not have "appropriate" paperwork. I *did* have all the teaching material I needed. It was a GCSE class. In the exam 80% of them got A grade and A-stars'.

Larissa wants to stress that she does not advocate anarchy. 'There must be a system - but an appropriate one.'

Carol Clubb

It is widely reported that office staff are friendly, helpful and polite. Carol is one of the people who make Grey Friars what it is, an institution with the feel of a family. She is a little bubbly lady that callers to the front desk met for nearly twenty years although nowadays she has moved to an upstairs office.

Carol remembers a happy childhood in an Essex army family. She left school at 16 and has few regrets that she had to work rather than study. It wasn't an issue for her that she did not go to college. 'I don't know of any of my friends going to college.'

She worked at a dental practice until she married and had her two children, a girl and a boy. She wasn't a sixties rebel. She took time out to raise her kids, but in her early thirties realised that she wanted to get back to work - not only for money but also for her quality of life. She started out doing reception at the dental practice, but that did not suit her family commitments. Chance brought her to Grey Friars. A friend of hers was a neighbour of the Grey Friars principal Enid Bishop. Enid asked over the garden fence one day if she knew of anyone looking for work for one day a week. The friend told Carol. That was over twenty years ago and she has stayed ever since, increasing to three days a week and being prepared to come in for longer when it was necessary and working in the evenings. Carol says, 'It was a bonus that in those days the office staff didn't work in the school holidays.'

After so many years at the front desk, Carole now works in the offices. She had spent most of her time facing the public until a couple of years ago she wanted to do something else. The sort of problems she deals with need a cool head. A typical problem: 13 swimming classes are scheduled for the first week of term, but the pool is closed for repairs so everyone has to be contacted and advised. She has to 'keep the information flowing.'

She has seen a lot of the major changes go through. 'It's a lot bigger than it was. There's also a lot more management staff.' She recalls the old way of enrolment, which took place over a week at the start of the autumn term. 'It might not have been so good for the students, but it was great fun for the staff!' Everyone was keyed up with the pressure and working long days to get the students enrolled. 'Lots more camaraderie. We worked 12 or 13 hours and had our breakfast, lunch and tea provided here. But from the public point of view queuing wasn't so good.' This enrolment system was discontinued many years ago in favour of a more open, ongoing enrolment system.

Present students enrol by letter, telephone, email or visiting the reception, any time throughout the summer and up to the start of the course. 'The bad old days' with a queue stretching round the building and tables in the hall for the various subjects have long gone, but Carol recalls it with affection.

Carol remembers her first interview 22 years ago: 'I had an interview with Mrs Bishop the principal and Mr Underwood the registrar who sat in armchairs. They didn't even ask me if I could type which I couldn't. First thing I had to learn was to type, you couldn't get a job here now if you couldn't operate a keyboard. Probably it wasn't so important then. There were other girls in the office who could type and I was doing reception work. Obviously once you can type you can do more jobs.'

What does she see has changed most? 'Oh, computers of course.' Carol is proficient with them now. 'I went up to Chelmsford with my line manager on a course. Nine years ago it was.' The use of computers has revolutionised office work.

'We hadn't used computers before. None of us had touched one before. We came back quite excited and told Alan Skinner what all this was about. The amount of paperwork that those computers can shift!' However, Carol can see a downside to the IT revolution. 'Because we have got the computers we are all more accountable. Because it is on the computer you can get a lot of figures. You have to keep proving yourself.' So she sees computers as a mixed blessing. 'There is far more audit paperwork than there ever used to be.'

On balance Carol comes down in favour of the changes. 'There is no longer the necessity to make cards for everything like we used to. Computers cut down on some of the mundane stuff. Like the enrolment cards all cut and folded by hand. Mundane things have been cut down with the flick of a switch.'

What has been lost? 'There isn't quite the cosy feel that there used to be when the staff was much smaller and they knew one another better. But the atmosphere has remained friendly.' Carol says her office colleagues are mainly women and they always get on.

'Obviously your funding comes from the figures and that is where the paper work comes in.' Carol likes the ease of information that computers give. She has been working for twenty years in the office and hopes to retire at sixty.

Sometimes she wonders why she stayed simply a clerical assistant. 'It's a good place to work. If you are happy where you are and it fits in with family there is no reason to go further. It has always been a family environment between staff and students. I think that is changing now because central and local government interferes more with adult education. There is more differentiation between exams and non-exams. We are much more aware of qualifications. I think that in the past we've always had a view that a dressmaking class or a creative writing class is as important as a class which has an exam at the end of it. I'm not sure that the government sees it like that.

We are much more aware of the business side of it than we were before. I think that does have an effect; there is lots more competition. There is a lot more going on for people than there was twenty years ago. We have to be more aware of that. That is trickling down. We are all much more aware of the finance side of it than we were before. That does have an effect.

In the past you would have a class that people would come to year in year out. I don't think that happens so much now. Students are evaluated and move on. That can be a good thing because it frees up space for other people to come in if different people want to join. You might have had people in dressmaking, for example, for years. We now have a good rate of new people coming to classes every year. Management are very good at not wanting to turn people away when they have money difficulties.'

Is there a gulf between management, students and staff and is it increasing? 'Yes, there is. Management have got so much more to deal with. The whole thing is much bigger than it used to be. Whereas it used to be top management and office staff there is more in between now; having said that they are very accessible. You can always go to see one of them. I have been here a long time. During that time there have been family crises. I have always had 100% support.'

For Carol that support counts for so much and is probably the reason she has stayed here for so long. 'Although the gulf may widen the support stays. One of the questions I sometimes ask myself - why am I a clerical assistant twenty years on? When you work with the public you learn things everyday. There isn't a ladder you have to climb here. You get trained in new things. You get supported. If you do your job to the best of your ability that is enough.'

Support services, such as catering, study facilities, a reference library, common rooms, and a wide range of educational and social activities enhance the life of an institution such as Grey Friars. Some of these services, however, are vital to people's ability to gain access to learning opportunities. One such service is the crèche which enables any age parents, carers or grandparents to attend class. The crèche has been a service offered to students for over thirty years. Allin Coleman the first principal started the service. The Grey Friars crèche now operates out of four rooms. Without its facilities most of the mothers (and a few fathers) would be unable to attend a course. There are over one hundred children and babies on the roll, cared for by 12 part-time and one full-time employee, who heads the team. The college opened a similar provision in 1999 at its annexe, the Wilson Marriage Centre.

Julie Walters

'This is such a happy place to work in,' says Julie, the Nursery manager and the only full-time staff member in that department. Although the nursery is not custom built, the rooms are adapted for small people and kept spotless. Each wall is covered with children's work, posters and pictures. In line with current nursery school practice there is a set theme each term. This term it is sport. The babies have their own cosy room with floor cushions and cuddly toys. The older children up to five years of age have the use of several other rooms. There has to be security, sadly, of course - you can only enter the crèche by stating your name and business on the intercom.

Julie proudly showed a small outdoor courtyard that will be used for swings and outdoor games once a soft surface is put down. This extends the opportunity for outdoor play and exploration.

Most of Julie's working life has been spent in childcare. She trained in a tough area of east London as a nursery nurse. Before she married she tried one year as a nanny in a wealthy St Johns Wood house. 'I enjoyed it,' she says. 'Tea at the Ritz and chauffeur driven cars.' But it wasn't something she clung to; she married and had four children and returned to nursery nursing. She has been at Grey Friars over twenty years. She notices how many of her staff have been working for several years at the crèche. 'The Grey Friars experience!' she smiles.

She is the sort of person who takes everything in her stride even the increase in paperwork which bothers many others. She accepts that there is more than when she first started, but believes most of it is necessary to ensure the smooth running of the service. 'I always ensure that I get to spend some sessions with children and if it is a choice between children or paper, children win every time.'

The children arrive at nursery from all walks of life and ethnic backgrounds; many are the children of parents for whom English is not their mother tongue, nor the language most usually spoken at home. These parents are also of varied nationalities and backgrounds, non-native speakers, asylum seekers and migrant workers.

'To be honest, in some circumstances it's easier sometimes to communicate with the children than their parents,' says Julie. 'We have developed ways to overcome this and usually get there in the end. Children will very readily use signs and body language and watch adults' facial expressions.' One Chinese boy commented to his Mum that Julie was always smiling.

The job can have its stresses. The inconsistencies of students' attendances can be worrying. Julie is aware of the multiple problems the students may have in attending regularly; sometimes, however, like the day of my visit, an assistant is waiting for three children who were expected, none of whom have turned up.

Julia is resigned to accepting that erratic attendance is one of the problems to cope with. But the prevalence of success stories puts the problems in perspective. Julie recalls one student with a difficult background of abuse whose children were taken into care. She had a baby who came to the nursery while her Mum joined a literacy class. When this student received an attendance certificate she showed it to Julie almost crying. It was the first recognition she had ever received for anything in her life. This woman is now reunited with her original children and is coping with her life. 'She gained self esteem and a feeling of worth,' says Julie, 'that is real success.'

Sometimes a student starts a course more than once before they are able to fully commit to study or find the right course for them. 'We smile, welcome them back and start again.' Julie's friendliness means a great deal to parents. One woman attending an Essential English class recently asked whether she would read the story she had written - the first one ever. 'A wonderful moment for her and me.'

Most children come for one two-hour session a week so Julie says that the emphasis in the nursery is on socialisation and learning through play. The ratio of staff to children is reassuringly high, the law insists on strict ratios at different ages. 'In practice,' Julie says, 'Our ratio is better.'

Julie is rightly proud of the benefits the crèche brings to both parents and children. The Institute of Education carried out a survey in 2004 and issued a report in the research series *The Benefits of Learning* (See chapter 9) which showed that when parents went out to study, their children broadened their range of social relationships at college crèches and playgroups. Many parents interviewed reported that studying any subject, even unconnected to parenting, made them more confident as parents, better able to communicate with their children and more understanding and patient. Julie says proudly that Grey Friars underwrites the funding of the nursery. 'The Governors have never put us under pressure about the costs of the service, although we are aware of the need to keep expenditure down and do what we can to work efficiently.' Students pay £5 a session, not anywhere near the real cost, and many of them are absolved from fees. She comments, 'Some parents attend a course to "get them out of the house" and then are bitten by the learning bug.'

Although this is essentially a service to support learners, there are definite advantages for the children's development (yet another contribution to society which is un-quantifiable in the present restrictive funding system). Children once used to the crèche will often refuse to leave.

A measure of the importance of the crèche (now fully registered with Ofsted as a day nursery and recipient of two excellent reports after inspection – neither of which leads to funding in the present system) is that in recognition of Julie's leadership of a fully committed team, principal Alan Skinner broke one of his own very firm rules. He has always been reticent to heap public praise on individuals rather than applaud team efforts. This year, however, he personally nominated Julie for a national award.

'I don't feel comfortable with the highly-publicised awards systems that are used to provide exemplars on a wide scale. I just can't see how those who most need the motivation can necessarily identify with the hype. But Julie's work is so important to the college ethos – and she transcends so many of the artificially imposed barriers of expertise that have come with the new regulation, inspection and audit regime – that I felt I had to make a point by highlighting the value of an all-rounder in an unsung role.' Julie did not make the national final, but her nomination for an award as an 'unsung hero' is testament to the value of her contribution to Grey Friars.   [DS]

TRADE NAMES:
Appearing throughout the years in the prospectus were tutors with ideal names for the job in hand

Dressmaking	Mrs CREES	1969
Swimming	Mr WALTER	1976
Family Cooking	Mrs BUTCHER	1977
Oil Painting	JOHN CONSTABLE	1979
Tailoring and dressmaking	Mrs P. VALLANCE	1982
Swimming	Mrs FINN	1984
Flower Arranging	Mrs GREEN	1984
French	Ms FRANCE Gaudy	2000

Teachers with other generally appropriate names were
Miss MARKHAM, Mr SCOLDING, Miss STERN and Mr CHALKLEY.

Italian: Senior Tutor Giovanni Gravina (centre) uses maps as a teaching aid.

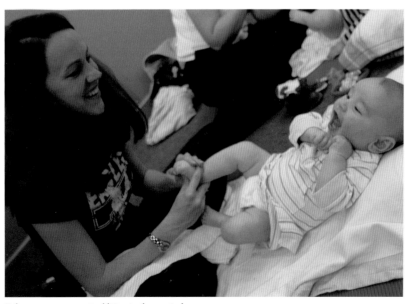

Baby massage: a recent addition to the curriculum.

Arts and crafts: the appeal of the wide range of courses transcends generations.

Ann Donnelly: long-serving tutor of art at all levels, including preparation for university entrance.

Keith Whitelock: from Grey Friars student to practising illustrator to tutor.

Howard Leyshon: the College's longest-serving art tutor.

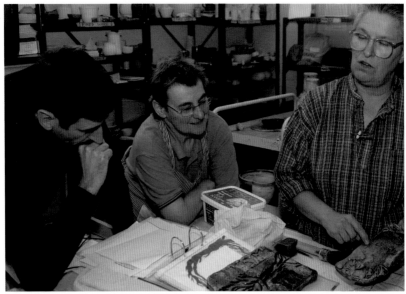

Ceramics: Barbara Wells (right) teaches courses from beginner level to City & Guilds qualifications.

Stained Glass: one of the many crafts taught by local practising professionals.

Sculpture: the studio at Wilson Marriage Centre.

Sculpture: work in progress in the studio.

Basic Skills: taught with relevance to adults' practical needs.

Creative Writing: tutor Dorothy Schwarz (centre) has published students' work.

Dance: courses include dancing from across the world.

Music: a range of courses encouraging everyone to participate.

Grey Friars accommodated the Lower School of the Colchester County High School in 1923.

Grey Friars as an adult college: staff, governors and volunteers in 1996.

Maths: work in progress - classes sometimes take the form of workshops.

Maths: students can follow individual programmes mapped to their needs.

Familiar corridors: generations have passed this way from the 1724 house to the school extension of 1903.

Reception: Registrar Jon Williams checks all is well with duty receptionist Julie Totman.

The 1755 extension: now screened off from the main stairwell due to safety regulations.

Hoist mechanism: still in situ in former servants' quarters.

Roofscape: original 1724 house (right) main stairwell dome (centre) and 1755 extension (left).

Hidden stairs: former servants' staircase, now unused, identifiable from angled floorboards and handrail.

Baby room: Grey Friars Nursery accommodates babies in a stimulating environment.

Toddler Room: Nursery staff encourage children to enjoy creative activities.

Drink-and-a-story time: Nursery Manager Julie Walters takes children through a story at breaktime.

Drink-and-a-chat time: Ursula's coffee bar snacks are served with a smile and a warm welcome.

New technologies: IT opportunities are now spreading across curriculum divisions.

In harmony: Bill Tamblyn's singing classes use music from across the world.

6

Skills

At the time of the establishment of the Learning and Skills Council (LSC) as the body for the planning and funding of all post-school education and training (except Higher Education) the Government set out its aims. Economic prosperity came first, but in his instructions to the LSC in the remit letter of November 2000, Education Secretary David Blunkett said 'Learning encourages people to develop as active citizens and to play a full part in their local community. It strengthens families, builds stronger neighbourhoods, helps older people to stay healthy and active and encourages independence for all by opening up new opportunities – including the chance to explore art, music and literature.'

The foreword to the Skills Strategy White Paper of 2003 was signed by the Prime Minister, Tony Blair, Education Secretary Charles Clarke, Trade and Industry Secretary Patricia Hewitt, Work and Pensions Secretary Andrew Smith and Chancellor of the Exchequer Gordon Brown, presumably as a demonstration of their desire for 'joined-up government'.

In a direct reference to education as a means of fostering economic prosperity the foreword states, 'Sustaining a competitive, productive economy which delivers prosperity for all requires an ever growing proportion of skilled, qualified people. We will not achieve a fairer, more inclusive society if we fail to narrow the gap between the skills-rich and the skills-poor.' However, they also acknowledged the wider value of learning: 'We must motivate and support many more learners to re-engage in learning. For too many people, learning is something which stops when they leave school. Learning new skills, at work and for pleasure, must become a rewarding part of everyday life.'

The LSC wanted to see an expansion of provision in the foundation skills of literacy and numeracy. Grey Friars staff planned programmes based not only on their professional academic knowledge, but also on their links to the community – researching, discussing and engaging a variety of agencies to support access to learning.

Important to the success of these programmes was belief that the learner is the focus of the activity, not the subject being 'taught'. This approach takes into account all aspects of the learning environment, including learners' previous experiences and, in the case of those with very basic skills needs, takes great care with the induction of new learners. The foundations for this were laid in the late 1980s.

The Open Learning Unit for Basic Skills

Where the needs of people with deep-rooted educational difficulties are concerned, the most sensitive and flexible approaches are required. That is exactly what concerned Grey Friars when Maggie Nutt was appointed to start its Open Learning Unit in 1989. This new aspect of Grey Friars' work was to be characterised by being individually focused, using diagnostic activities and fitting in with people's own timescales. Learners were encouraged to move to a class only when they had received sufficient one-to-one support and, where necessary, such support continued once they had joined a class. The location of the Unit next to the front door was essential. It was also directly opposite the main reception and enrolment area, so Maggie could personally introduce her new learners to the College processes.

The College was able to embark upon this ambitious project as a result of a successful bid for government funding, prepared and supported by the LEA's local specialist officer in adult basic education, Sue Abell. Not only did Sue robustly pursue a successful outcome to the bid, but also gave a great deal of her professional and personal time to seeing it through to fruition. A key element in the success of the bid was securing a statement from the LEA at the end of the bid document, saying 'Essex County Council is committed to the continuation of the project'.

Maggie came to the College with a firm belief, reached through years of experience, that there was no one definitive approach to encouraging adults to face up to their basic skills difficulties. Neither is there any single way of tackling those difficulties and overcoming them. 'There still seemed to be in many quarters an attitude that literacy problems, especially, were peculiar to a certain section of society. In other words, a person could be defined as "a typical basic skills student". The College believed that this was patently wrong and I shared that belief,' she said. 'Acquisition of adequate literacy and numeracy skills has proved to be difficult for a wide range of people from all parts of society. Not all of those problems are caused by lack of academic skills, or lack of intelligence. Health and social issues can have interrupted the educational development of many adults and we are now able to find more specific reasons, such as dyslexia.'

Stories of people who attended early in the life of the Unit, as well as many who came to Grey Friars subsequently, illustrate a wide range of reasons and motivations. (In this section, due to the sensitive nature of some people's circumstances, the names have been changed.)

Andrea, who had to contend with a number of mental health issues, would clearly never have had so smooth and supportive an introduction to the College had she not been able to be met by someone who not only would welcome her, but also engage immediately in the task of sensitively assessing her educational needs. Maggie was able to engage from the very beginning in a totally student-centred analysis of Andrea's learning requirements and, being an experienced member of the tutorial staff, was also able to take account of and advise colleagues on those needs. This enhanced the quality of Andrea's learning. One of the Unit's major contributions to Grey Friars was the induction of new, sometimes reticent, sometimes very apprehensive basic skills learners.

Barbara had been struggling with her education, which had been made more difficult for her by a hearing impairment and an associated speech impediment. She presented herself to Maggie as someone who was lacking ability, but it soon became apparent – again, through the one-to-one relationship and relaxed diagnostic processes – that she was very able indeed. There was now a dedicated professional who had time for Barbara, could cope with her 'popping in' and could arrange a flexible learning programme, just for her. She went on to overcome many of her learning problems, gained a job with the probation service and Maggie recalls her sincere appreciation: 'You started me off – I'll never forget that'.

Carrie knew she could achieve more in her life and recognised that getting to grips with the basic skills of reading, spelling and writing would lay the foundations for her improvement. She began what was to become a long trail of gradual progression by focusing on her craft skills in a City & Guilds course. With the support of Maggie and colleagues during her craft course and continued attendance at English classes, she became confident enough to enrol at Writtle Agricultural College. She came back to Grey Friars for further assistance and was able to give something back by helping adults with severe learning difficulties with their craft courses. Carrie now works full-time in supporting adults with disabilities in their horticultural activities. Maggie remembers a comment from Carrie which highlighted a valuable associated effect: she felt that her children's successful educational performance may very well have stemmed from seeing their mother as a committed learner.

David is an enthusiastic advocate of adult learning as a result of his time with Grey Friars. A family man in his 30s, he was a stalwart learner, cycling into town from a local village in all seasons and attending evening classes regularly. Maggie remembers him as a man with great application to the task: 'He showed a wonderful sense of realism, accepting that although progress was slow, it was still positive. When I had to advise him that he wasn't ready for the examination, he cheerfully said, "That's alright Maggie, I'll come again – and keep coming." He was working as a carer and desperately wanted to become a nurse. He needed five GCSEs including Maths and English.' Maggie remembers feeling 'thrilled' when he finally telephoned to tell her he had been accepted for nurse training. He now works at the General Hospital. 'I'd tell anyone how it changed my life for the better,' David told Maggie.

Edward's personal situation and lifestyle could not have been more different. A wealthy man who had his own company, Edward was able only to write his name. Once he had met Maggie, he told her of the many 'false starts' – driving round and round the area, eventually approaching Grey Friars, 'hovering and hesitating' - only to go away again. He had a supportive family and had set himself two main targets: to be able to 'read an airport novel' and to write postcards from his holiday home in the sun. Maggie says: 'His huge motivation, coupled with the flexibility we could give him in his learning resulted in him eventually sending me a postcard, all his own work - that was a moving moment for me.'

Cultural and lifestyle issues featured in Freddie's case. A traveller living on a local council official site, he first heard of Grey Friars' services when staff visited families on the site to give tuition. However, he preferred to attend Grey Friars in order to preserve his anonymity and Maggie soon found that one-to-one tuition was imperative for Freddie. The lack of any culturally-relevant teaching materials led to them making a book of his day-to-day life, in order to use it as source material for the lessons. When asked how an Open Learning Unit approach would fit in today, Maggie was convinced that it would still make a valid contribution. Despite the vastly-increased government funding now available, the high-profile 'gremlins' advertisements on television, the national help-lines and financial incentives for employers, many people will still slip through the net.

'Today's money comes with so many strings attached. I feel very strongly that the present need to relate so much of the work in basic skills to a national curriculum and national tests can sometimes be restrictive' she says. Maggie shares the grave concerns of many adult educators as to how some of their successful students of the past, exemplified by the Open Learning Unit stories, would have reacted to the highly-audited, form-filling culture which is now necessary to guarantee that the work remains publicly-funded. Many staff feel that people whose potential for further learning was dramatically released by conquering basic skills problems may never have achieved eventual academic success had it not been for the individual needs-centred, non-pressurised induction they received from the Unit when they first came to Grey Friars.

'I always was very doubtful about the increasing prevalence of formal testing, but colleagues have told me that they believe many advantages have come from the national curriculum and assessment methods. Fair enough, I can accept that, but I feel that basic education specialists should never lose sight of the relevance of individual needs – not all of which will fit neatly into categories that can be audited. We should take as much care of the small number of people with multiple reasons for not having gained skills as we do of the majority who can relate to the modern quick-fix methods, for example through the use of computers. Perhaps we should take even greater care of the former, as the majority march forward and the minority are left further behind.

'Short-term funding and brief high-profile campaigns mean that there may not be sustainability for those for whom rapid progress, or even any progress, is difficult to make. It would also help if funding authorities showed greater faith in the professionals, allowing them to judge the best way to engage people locally and individually. It is understandable that the government felt it necessary to take a nationwide view of the issue, but it has been very frustrating for those of us who had already worked so hard to increase access, raise quality, train staff professionally and maintain relevance to our local communities – well before the funding increased to present levels.'

In the light of Maggie's reference to 'short-term funding' a related story gives a further example of the Grey Friars approach. The County Council commitment in the bid for funding stated that the work of the Open Learning Unit would be continued beyond the two-year government-funded period. It was, but not with direct LEA funds.

Upon hearing the news that unfortunately the LEA was unable to fulfil its committment to support the Unit once the government money ran out, the College response was to find a way to continue the work. To withdraw a learning support system that had been proved to work, and would have left people part-way through programmes would have been a retrograde step. The immediate action taken was to increase income from running the car park as a business to pay for taking Maggie on as a permanent member of staff. So Maggie became the first member of the teaching staff at Grey Friars to be added to the payroll courtesy of income from car park fees for public parking. It is worth noting that that these measures would not have been possible if the car park had not previously been established as a business in order to cope with earlier funding problems arising from national and local government cuts in the mid-1980s.

1992-3, however, saw the greatest damage to the Open Learning Unit's contribution when, in reaction to the Further and Higher Education Act, Essex County Council reorganised its adult education services and moved staff around to fit the new system. Maggie Nutt was to spend half of her time in Tendring and was no longer as available as before. Although the totally person-centered approach had been compromised, the College kept what it could of the Open Learning Unit's style.

Basic skills staff to this day continue to be appreciative of learners' individual needs and the College makes every effort to be as welcoming as before. This is the case throughout the basic skills programme, no more so than when English is being taught as a second language.   [AS]

Grey Friars offers over fifty courses in English for non-native speakers who are UK residents. The teaching of these courses is undertaken by seven women and one male tutor. ESOL courses come within the remit of Skills for Life and are non-fee paying. Specialist courses began in the early 1970s on a national level.

The government set targets to improve literacy and numeracy skills and all courses are funded nationally. There are now national curricula in English, numeracy and English as a second language. All tutors have to be trained and qualified in the national curriculum for their subject.

The aim of these courses is to help citizens improve their communication, maths or English skills. They also aim to help plug a gap in a CV or prepare the student to take a national test.

Maria Mackenzie

Maria, in her early thirties, is very content with her work as an ESOL tutor. Like so many of the tutors who teach adults, she joined further education later in her career. She experienced Grey Friars as a teenage student, as a mature student and now as a part time tutor. She left home young and travelled abroad for a while, before returning to the UK and taking a variety of jobs. As a student in her twenties, she came to Grey Friars and joined an Access planning course. This led to, at twenty-six, being accepted at Essex University to read languages as a mature student.

'I thought that it was a good age to study. I've done lots of classes here over the years. It's been a stepping-stone for me. I did a French A Level at Grey Friars before I went back to university. I never took the exam but it was a great help.'

Now that Maria has her degree, she prefers the higher level of freedom that part-time teaching gives her. She still joins Grey Friars as a student and is studying an advanced level non-exam French culture course. She loves it. 'It is lifelong learning - a class like that.'

Maria sees the variety of courses as a positive aspect of Grey Friars, 'The choice of classes is fantastic. Things are taught now that weren't even thought of before.'

She says, 'Also, I don't like the paperwork. But I have to say that sometimes it will force me to prepare a detailed scheme of work, which is useful. On the other hand, this often needs to be tailored for students once

I've met them'. She hasn't fully made up her mind about the usefulness of the many forms to fill in. 'Sometimes the paperwork is the bane of my life, but I can find short cuts.' It is the senior management staff who have to insist that this new level of paperwork is adhered to. But Maria, in common with most tutors, doesn't find that it sours her relationship with them. There is a consistent high level of support running from the managers to the tutors and back again.

Maria's Tuesday class of ESOL Pre-Intermediate students runs for a full academic year. The group comprises only women, half of them Bangladeshi, ranging in age from twenty to sixty. Two of the older women had lived in Colchester for over thirty years. They were great friends and their husbands also. Their families had made a success of moving to the UK from Sylhet in Bangladesh and their children, they told me proudly, had entered the professions, one girl was a GP, one son a lawyer. Their husbands on retirement would like to return to Bangladesh, but they would not. As Salema said, 'Our children live here.' These two older Bangladeshi women exuded a quiet self confidence whereas the younger Bangladeshi women were more shy and hesitant to speak English.

Two women in the class, one from Japan and one from Cuba, were there because they had married English men and wanted to improve their spoken language. Marlene from Cuba also wanted English to improve her work situation, although Junke from Japan did not want to work here. The majority of the group told me that they enjoyed living in Colchester, although one woman from Teheran said that she and her daughter aged eleven could not wait to go home.

I asked the students if there was anything that they didn't like about Grey Friars and there was laughter. The only complaints were too many stairs and not enough room in the car park on busy days. Praise from the students was universal. They were more than satisfied with the teaching and support at Grey Friars, considering the tutors friendly and the atmosphere supportive. The young Bengali women said that coming to Grey Friars even once a week helped them to gain confidence.

Maria is teaching with a volunteer who has been at Grey Friars since she retired from the Civil Service in 1984. She herself had been at school at Grey Friars sixty years ago when it was still a girl's school. She recalls cycling through the playground (now the car park) and being scolded by the strict head mistress. With the increasing demand for qualifications, volunteers may soon be required to have a teaching qualification like a City and Guilds Part One certificate. This volunteer says crossly that if and when that situation arises, she will regretfully cease volunteering.

Maria handed out the homework – a text about the meaning of home. The students were to add their comments. There was an atmosphere of friendliness and cooperation in the group. These are women who want learning for its own sake rather than for a qualification. They are learning to improve their quality of life.

Julie Burgess

Like many of the tutors we met, Julie came into Adult Education from a non-professional background. 'My cousin and I,' she says, 'are the first in our family to go to college.' Her parents wanted her to leave school, encouraging her towards the 'safety' of a bank-clerk career. 'I wouldn't have been happy working in a bank,' she says.

She took a degree in German, inspired by the brilliant language tuition of her teacher in high school. After her degree, she wanted to teach English as a foreign language (TEFL) but didn't have the money to fund herself. So she worked in industry for a couple of years, saved enough and paid for the course. After teaching TEFL in London and Cambridge, she made a career shift sideways, did a post-graduate certificate in education (PGCE) that took her into secondary school teaching.

Gradually she moved into part-time teaching in adult education. One course leads to another as many part-time tutors find. Now, she takes half a dozen classes in the languages, ESOL and family learning departments. She makes a modest living and enjoys the work; she intends to stay in it for the next few years at least. 'Coming from a school environment,' she says, 'I find people are friendly and the students attentive. I needed that.'

Sometimes lack of funding can cause difficulties. On one occasion, she had to buy a text book herself at a cost of £50, although she had no guarantee that the class would run. Numbers of students must be kept to eight at least and some classes have been closed due to low enrolments or drop-outs. She also worries that there isn't enough access to computers, but at least there are always enough tape recorders and television sets.

In Julie's present ESOL pre-examination class there are only five students and thus the class may have to close. Unlike Maria's group of mainly Asian women, who are studying English as life enrichment, the five students in Julie's class are from Eastern Europe. Migrants wishing to improve their economic status, they need English for work. One of the students from Ukraine is a qualified doctor, as is her husband. Both work as carers in an old persons' home, sending most of their salaries back home for the support of the four year-old child they have left with Granny; they hope to amass enough capital to buy a house in Ukraine. A Polish student was here taking a year out from his pharmaceutical studies in Warsaw. He finds that he can live quite easily in Colchester on a hospital housekeeper's wage, but he was indignant that his English conversation class had been cancelled due to low enrolment.

For Julie, taking this class through the grammar exercises was both easy and pleasant. Grey Friars holds a special place in her heart for quite another reason. Like many Grey Friars tutors she also studies here. On a short story course recently she met Mr Budd, a Colchester Borough Council employee. Two years later, she is now Mrs Budd.

The 'Skills for Life' department

Carolyn Roberts is one of two Curriculum Managers with a full time post, responsible for Curriculum Area 14. This includes Outreach, Learning Difficulties, Skills for Life (the new national term for literacy and numeracy), Additional Learning Support and Family Learning. These are areas where Grey Friars supports families and many others who have dropped out of the educational race and need training either as a job preparation or simply to improve the quality of their life.

Carolyn like many Grey Friars tutors came late in her career to Adult Education, bringing many years of outside experience to the task. She was born in Chelmsford. She worked in industry with Ford Motor Company for five years. But she wanted something more challenging and started a travel business with a friend in 1987. The business was a great success - hardly a surprise with someone like Carolyn running it - and when after a few years she was bought out by a major corporation, Townsend

Thoresen, she stayed on as a consultant.

'After a year I decided on a sabbatical and went to teach in Hungary,' she says. The one year stretched into eight fascinating years where she learned the Hungarian language, partook of its rich culture and ended up after a spell at the Agricultural University in Budapest, teaching English. 'I'm not political,' she says, 'but the culture fascinated me.' Carolyn kept up her British links by teaching a summer school in Harlow. Her next decision is familiar to all working mums, she dropped out to have her son. 'I didn't want to miss out.'

However, during these years she gained more academic qualifications. Since 1995 she says, 'I have gained at least one or two additional qualifications each year. It is so important to keep up to date and on top of it all.'

Carolyn points out that the whole methodology of teaching basic skills has changed. There is a thrust to professionalise the service. Most senior staff will agree with this and accept the moving goal posts. With the need to train an increasingly better qualified work force to compete on global levels, colleges will seek younger applicants. This in itself is no bad thing but care must be taken to include adult learners.

Many adults in Carolyn's department are 35-40 year olds who wish to enhance their skills. The level of motivation within such a class is totally different from that of 16-18 year olds who may be obliged to attend courses. Carolyn points out that adults 'come to the classroom with more experience. Youngsters have a different perspective on life.' The database shows the present age breakdown for literacy and numeracy classes comprises 5% under-19s and 83% 19-59s. Learners aged 60-plus form 10% of the student body in this department.

Family Learning

Family Learning courses aim to get families involved in helping their children achieve well at school. A welcome side-effect of parents entering their children's school situation is that they themselves may benefit.

Carolyn says, 'We get the whole spectrum of learning because of the school curriculum.' Courses may run for a day or an evening or a few weekly sessions. One successful course on budgeting (described later in this chapter) has led to a three-term course in an outreach centre.

Carolyn has approached the concept of education in the widest sense possible within the available resources. She believes in putting fun and enjoyment together with learning skills or gathering information. For Family Learning Week, the team put on a circus skills course, which ran very successfully with 60 participants.

A similar scheme, based on football skills for adults and children used Colchester United Football Club as a partner to provide the expertise. The first football skills course took place at Thomas Lord Audley Comprehensive over an October weekend. Youngsters were given football skills training and the adults were also able to make use of the College's mobile classroom which provided IT sessions. Parents used the computer to put their score sheets into charts and graphs, learning how to do that with their child. Other family activities ranged from a puppet-making weekend to the Bangladeshi Ladies Committee organizing a sari weekend. These ladies would likely not have had the confidence to do this were it not for the background support that the Family Learning scheme had given them.

The sort of activity that Carolyn believes is essential for Family Learning is one where multi-tasking can be utilised. She cites the ride-a-bike course as an example. The participants had to construct their own bicycle using mathematical skills; eight students completed the course and got the bike at the end. She funded this course by applying for a short-term grant from the Learning Skills Council.

In another initiative, the mobile classroom goes to the bus station each week for the use of the employees of First Group bus company. In this scheme they improve their IT skills. Approaching 100 employees over a three-year period have availed themselves of this opportunity.

Carolyn organizes the core programmes which are printed in the brochure and on the College's website, but she also has sidelines such as those outlined above. She is innovative and enthusiastic: 'We have to bid for funds and come up with new ideas.' Carolyn sees her job as finding out what the community wants, assessing the need and then providing what is required.

The funding for Skills for Life activities is at present quite generous in comparison to the rest of the curriculum, as central government has prioritised this work. These funds are used for both literacy, numeracy and English language classes as well as to provide extra-curricula courses geared to family needs. The basic literacy, numeracy and English language courses have always been an essential and respected part of Grey Friars' work. As Carolyn points out, 'Having the foundation of basic learning makes an enormous difference in a person's life. Seeing that happen is very rewarding for me.'

She gives many examples. 'We have had deaf people come to us with minimal skills. After a time here they have often gained a skill, got a qualification and obtained a job. Primarily because they were deaf they'd lacked the confidence to find out what they were entitled to. She cites the case of a young man of 18, with a low level of skills. 'We arranged a sign language interpreter for him. Over time he managed to get both a job and his own accommodation. Now aged 22, he has grown immeasurably in self confidence.'

Carolyn has three other full-time managers in her area and twenty-three part-time tutors run the courses. Two of Carolyn's team of part time tutors Richard Cooper and Eric Melvin, both of whom have come in to adult education later in life from commercial and industrial backgrounds, love the work and want to stay with it to the end of their working lives.

Adults with Learning Difficulties

Richard Cooper is a remarkable communicator in his early 50s who has been senior tutor for adults with learning difficulties for the last 15 months.

He was born in London and had an unsettled childhood moving often because his father was in the forces. Raised in Ripon, Yorkshire and ultimately in Chelmsford, he left school at fifteen with no formal qualifications. He went into retail business and began to working in sales promotion as a member of the display team. His lack of formal qualifications was no barrier in those days, unlike now. Richard followed a 'work based training programme', first at Burton's menswear, later moving on to become area display manager for a local menswear company. During the following years, Richard became involved in voluntary work at a local school, assisting on youth theatre workshops and performances. This, in turn, led to a similar role at the local college, working with adults with learning disabilities. It became something of a passion for Richard to pass on his own experience of using drama as a confidence builder to those in this area of learning.

The closure of the menswear company led to redundancy in the early nineties - a turning point in his life. It was at this time that Richard took up regular employment in residential homes for adults with learning difficulties. He worked in a rural residential care home in an idyllic setting in the country, but he grew increasingly aware that although personal care needs were met, there was not enough community access and social interaction for his clients. He moved on to a new residential home, where he became a part of the management team as the 'Community Support Manager' co-ordinating a weekly timetable for the residents, addressing educational and social issues.

Liaising with adult education colleges, he found there were already suitable courses for clients such as his. Over twenty courses could help about one hundred adults in an academic year.

By now Richard realised that he himself needed formal qualifications in order to give educational support to learning-disabled people, so he took the City and Guilds Teacher Training Certificate Parts One and Two at Colchester Institute. At present he is completing a Certificate in Education. Although he finds the formalising into academic language of skills that he has already been practising for years can be irksome, he sees the value of the course. He feels particularly fortunate that he has had the same tutor throughout - Marion Williams, also a Grey Friars tutor and a governor.

Grey Friars offered him the opportunity in September 2003 to take charge of all the courses offered in his field, on the understanding that he completed the Cert Ed. Richard is now running around fifty courses for adults with learning difficulties. The courses are non-fee paying with the cost borne from the Grey Friars budget.

Richard believes that the friendly environment at Grey Friars and the Wilson Marriage Centre is appropriate for this area of learning as many of the students find larger institutions like Colchester Institute and Braintree College intimidating; they can be forbidding both from the outside and on the inside. This is certainly not the case with Grey Friars or Wilson

Marriage. Most of the classes were only 6-8 people so the interaction between tutor and students in the group can be more enriching. Social interaction during break times is an integral part of the sessions. Richard's background in residential care has provided an invaluable foundation for his current role. He endeavours to maintain a friendly and supportive relationship with the students and at the same time, liase comfortably with carers and families.

Since beginning his work at Grey Friars, Richard has networked the Colchester area and discovered that there are many people with extremely complex needs who were not accessing college. They may be living in a small group home with only three or four residents, doing little more than sitting in front of a TV that they are not really watching. Richard wanted to encourage them to engage positively with their surroundings and fulfil their potential to participate, not observe.

Richard devised the idea of a sensory course to offer stimulation, which materialised after meeting and subsequently employing a tutor from Wakes Hall called Sharron Howard who loved his idea and developed it into a course called "Touchy Feely". The students use many different materials to create a piece of artwork. This concept of devising a class to stimulate tactile and visual sense has been so successful that two have run and more are planned.

Richard is convinced of the value of this work at Grey Friars. He says, 'There are a lot of people living in the community whose quality of life can be improved by accessing college. Those with a higher level of ability, who live independently with minimal support often call at the college. Living alone, they may suffer isolation and just want to talk. Another innovative class called "Speak for Yourself" involves the students' choice of issues where they can discuss and share their experiences at their own level. 'As the class tutor, I endeavour to take a step back and allow the students themselves to do most of the talking.'

According to present directives from government, all courses must be matched to the 'National Skills for Life Pre-Entry Curriculum' which, although it means a lot of extra work for tutors, has the benefit of progression routes being monitored and meticulously recorded. Some students then move up to 'Entry Level 1'.

Richard interviews all prospective students and is motivated by following their progress and observing the interaction that takes place, both in the classroom and in social terms such as 'end of term' events and parties. On Thursday evenings at the Wilson Marriage Centre any students and their friends can take part in a social get-together. The atmosphere is purposeful with plenty of fun and laughter.

Outreach

One of Grey Friars' most important commitments is work outside the normal educational environment. Eric Melvin is one of the most popular tutors in this field.

He came south in his late teens and had a thirty-year career in industry. Taking early retirement at the age of fifty, he began to fulfil a lifelong desire to teach. As a manager for Iceland he'd always enjoyed the training aspect of his work. His expertise is in maths. Gaining the necessary qualifications of City and Guilds Stages 1 and II in Adult Education, he started teaching a couple of courses in the Family Learning department. Now, two years later, he teaches eight courses a week and is honing his own skills by taking an IT course. He works well with Carolyn Roberts who heads the department. Having been a manager himself for many years he knows the score. 'She took a risk with me,' he says, referring to her willingness to see the potential in his skills although he came from another sector. He enjoys this second career. 'I am staying. I would not want to become a manager again.'

Does he not mind that the salaries are lower in teaching than in industry? Not really he says. He agrees that if you consider the time preparing your materials which isn't paid for, the salaries are relatively low. But he accepts this because of how much he enjoys the contact with students. And preparation grows easier with each successful course. 'Once I have gathered the material together, I can use the previous year's resources.' In Holy Trinity Primary School in Eight Ash Green, a fifteen-week course is in its second week. It is an open plan school so Eric and his group of adult learners occupy one end of an open space brightly decorated with pupil artwork. The students are all women ranging in age from late twenties to early forties. There are eight registered and all of them have done one or two courses with Eric already. On the day I visited there were four women attending. The course teaching parents how to help their children with maths has been tremendously popular.

This fifteen-week course is designed around managing the family budget, but the students will also learn how to use the Excel programme. Eric tells his students, 'When you've all finished you'll all have become computer operators and much more marketable when you go out for jobs.' He says that with a laugh, but it is what he absolutely believes in: that these family learning courses bring back into the education system people who possibly dropped out young and are diffident about entering again. He explains how intimidating it can be for a person who maybe left formal education years ago to start any academic subject or qualification. Starting a course designed to help you as a parent help your own child can be the way back. It can and does often lead to further studies.

This was borne out by speaking to the students. Suzanne has four kids and has no intention of working until the youngest is at secondary school. Not only because she wants to be a full time mum but also because in the low pay sector most of whatever wages she earns would go in childcare. She left school at 16 and had her first baby soon after. School wasn't a happy experience for her. But she says that these family learning courses are quite different. She feels her brain is being used. It's a way back for her and she has a goal – to become a midwife. She explains how a course like the Family Learning helps someone in her position gain in confidence.

Tracey, a little older, was pleased that Grey Friars had come to the primary school and provided the course on site – and also provided a crèche for two hours. 'It's knowing where to start that's difficult,' she says.

The women all agreed that the social aspect of such a course, being together, discussing problems, drinking tea meant so much to them. 'I'm not so alone anymore,' said one. 'Now I know where to go for help.' [DS]

A Special Needs class

We're in a tall green room at Wilson Marriage Centre. It's narrow and arranged lengthways, with a single row of tables facing the whiteboard and the teacher's desk. There's a high window that lets in ample light. This is where Anita Higgs runs her Pottery and Craft courses on Thursdays.

On a sunny March morning her students (there are six in the class) troop in gradually, mostly accompanied by helpers. Anita welcomes them and they take their seats. The atmosphere's very relaxed; one student shows off her engagement ring. She's in a wheelchair with a head support, and doesn't have use of her hands; nor can she clearly vocalize, though her helper can understand her. But she can communicate with her wide bright eyes.

Anita settles her students to a task. Last week they made small clay plaques, with patterns of dark clay inlaid into white; today they have to link them so that they can hang them up as an ornament. Anita allows them to choose how to do it, whether with green string or with white, and explains that they need to put the string through the holes in the plaques and fasten the pieces, which she cuts for them, with a knot.

It's obvious that she understands the capabilities of every student, and is setting out to extend them, helping them with their physical manipulation, their ability to interact socially and their aesthetic responsiveness – and giving them a sense of real achievement. One student keeps everything that he has made in her classes in his room in the home where he lives.

Then Anita sets the class to making Easter cards. She has a pack of coloured card, a bag of vivid dyed feathers, all oranges and yellows, blues and reds; she has cotton wool for making lambs, and bright felt-tips and glitter. She also prepared shapes for the students to colour and glue to their cards – churches and butterflies. There are flowers to cut out too. She listens to what each student wants to do, and helps them achieve their aim – there's a moment of humour as she puzzles out how to draw a rabbit on the board (pottery is her subject, rather than drawing). And all the time she's making supportive comments: 'That's much nicer, Karen,' or, 'Do you want me to outline your rabbit, Christine?' She's very capable and caring, a former mental nurse, relaxed, well-organised and confident in what she's able to achieve with her students.

All the students have 'Happy Easter' written on their cards – some can write it for themselves, some need to have it written for them. Some write personal messages: the lively young man makes his card for his girlfriend, finding a heart design to copy from a craft book, and needing just 'Easter' spelled out for him; the woman in the wheelchair gets her helper to write a long message to her fiancée. Sometimes the helper has recourse to a spelling board, when she can't understand; b-a-b-y, the woman spells out. She can paint using a head brace, though she doesn't use this skill in today's class.

Anita makes use of seasonal events. It is March 17th, St Patrick's Day, and she puts on a CD of Irish music. In a previous class the students made kites to celebrate the Chinese New Year – the results are on display, vivid brilliant fishes, extraordinarily attractive. So many fresh ideas.

Results of past projects hang on the walls. There are bright Mexican-style painted clay beads. 'Nearly all the students can do threading,' Anita says. There's a red wool man, a cork Father Christmas. One week the students did fabric-painting. Two women painted scarves, and wore them for weeks afterwards. The lively young man painted a tee-shirt, and his trousers. Today he's wearing a Manchester United shirt; 'I'm a supporter!' he says.

The craft room opens off the coffee bar, and at break-time the social experience of the class spills over into that space. The students have to buy their drinks and snacks themselves, good practice in the use of money, and the maths involved. They seat themselves around a table. Anita shows me detailed records of each student's achievements.

The students in her afternoon class are more vocal. It's obvious as she greets them that she knows them well – she remembers their projects and their ailments, even the musical taste of an Abba fan. There's plenty of laughter and teasing, the opportunity to work on pet projects. One man is making a quilt for a friend's baby and has appliquéd gingham hearts to the cover.   [MF]

Maggie Bernstein

Maggie, who has held various posts as teacher and senior tutor at Grey Friars, writes:

'Even though it was over twenty years ago, I still vividly remember my first visit to Grey Friars College and my subsequent enjoyment of the Painting and Drawing course that I had enrolled on. The class tutor had endless patience, always providing us with something interesting to draw and paint and talking knowledgeably about every aspect of Fine Art. It was a revelation.

Tutors at Grey Friars then and now teach mixed ability classes without patronising their students, and because of the large programme for adults with learning disabilities the college's public areas are a mixed ability social event too. I have worked at Grey Friars for ten years and my first impression has been reinforced over and over again. Colleagues work hard to retain the familial atmosphere without compromising their professional attitudes to the learning process.

Recently a colleague invited us to his students' (with learning disabilities) production of the "Wizard of Oz" at the Wilson Marriage Centre. The students, who possibly for the first time in their lives had an opportunity to be stars, acted their socks off and the audience participated throughout with much well earned applause. It was the most endearing, entertaining and gratifying half an hour at work I've enjoyed for a long time. At the end of the performance the tutor announced that he could now tick the boxes on his teaching assessment form that asked if the students had made progress in their learning, but as he pointed out, there is no tick box for student enjoyment.

With the swingeing cuts that we are now experiencing due to the LSCs change in emphasis, I'm wondering how many learners with disabilities, and also those without, will get the chance to experience a college that has for so many years created an atmosphere in which people feel they can safely admit a lack of knowledge, can increase their knowledge, learn new skills, develop as people and socialise with everyone.

What struck me about the "Wizard of Oz" was that perhaps those that determine our future need the same things as the Tin Man, the Lion and the Scarecrow and possibly, like the Wizard, need to admit that they aren't truly wizard at all. The Wizard of Oz did the right thing in the end and Dorothy got home. I can only hope that Grey Friars, like Dorothy, can survive all the setbacks.'

IT as an essential skill

At one time, if there was a man in a typing class, people wondered why he was there. Often, he would be a union representative, paid to attend in order to sharpen up his ability to write notes and deal with his own correspondence. Other men have included writers or owners of small businesses. However, the number of men increased rapidly when those interested in computers wanted to increase their 'keyboarding skills'. Now the adult education gender balance (75% female) is being seriously challenged.

As the college gets to grips with the 21st century, traditional teaching methods have been modified. Indeed, no department has had to change as much as office studies – subjects, syllabuses, teaching styles, recruitment methods, progression routes, course timings, support services, staff training, exams, classroom facilities have all required new approaches. And with the increasing need for every part of the college to address IT developments, the department has needed to integrate with other colleagues like never before.

As the college staff development strategy originally stated: 'The college will develop its staff in line with its own development as an institution.' The cross-college IT strategy group receives all the computer development funding for the whole college and decides collectively on priorities and the staff development organisers offer IT themes relevant to all staff throughout the year.

Co-operation and collaboration also take place in a much wider context. Grey Friars is a member of the Colchester Learning Shop partnership and is careful to collaborate with other institutions in planning programmes. With a subject area as fast-moving as IT, especially with the government pushing to make as many people 'IT literate' as possible, un-coordinated presentation of opportunities outside a strategic framework could lead to a free-for-all amongst providers. An inevitable result would be competition for funding, competition for students, disjointed routes of progression and worse still, confusion for the local people. In such a rapidly-changing subject area there must be a clear range of entry points, a coherent set of continuation opportunities and a well-documented route to higher-level study. The Learning Shop partnership, with its finger on the pulse of local needs, is the ideal forum for collaborative planning.

We need to understand why people want to learn – as well as what puts them off. As Marion said in chapter 3, 'These days, you don't have a job for life, a lot of people are burnt out by the time they are 40 or 45 or even 50. Knowing that you can re-train in an environment such as this is very important. Again, it's having that goal, having that ambition, and it doesn't stop just because you happen to have attained a certain age, you've still got more ambitions, you've still got other things you want to do'.

An understanding of the complicated nature of adult lives, fears and ambitions, together with a knowledge of local demographics, allows resources and expertise to be combined for an integrated solution. That is how the open-access IT Learning Centres at the college's Wilson Marriage Centre and at the Learning Shop itself were made possible. The Colchester Institute and Grey Friars collaborated to develop these alternatives to classroom courses – but with cross-reference in their programmes and an integrated advice and information service for student progression. Unfortunately, they were not aware of centres being planned by providers coming in from outside the area which came onto the market in a blaze of special offers and prize draws – immediately coming into open competition with the existing provision.

The LSC's pursuit of high targets for participation in the new National Literacy and Numeracy Tests has encouraged the newcomers to broaden their remit to include these basic skills. However, their students are usually 'taught' as well as tested via their IT equipment, with staff mainly facilitating, not teaching. This may be sufficient for learners who already have confidence and simply wish to 'brush up' their basic skills and take a test to add to their CV, but such an approach is unlikely to be suitable for those with more fundamental difficulties. It is incumbent upon the LSC, which has a planning role as well as a funding function, to ensure that there are strategies in place to maximise the effectiveness of all resources. If it ensures that information, advice and guidance systems used to publicise activities and recruit to them address learners' needs as well as the Government targets, there is a greater possibility of people accessing provision suitable for them and not just making up the numbers.

The greatest disappointment suffered by the Grey Friars IT department has not been anything to do with their own or their students' performances – indeed both have responded energetically to the technological and educational challenges. It has been in the arena of interinstitutional politics where they believe opportunities have been missed.

Long-standing members of staff, who prefer not to be named, said with resigned sighs, 'We spend a lot of time explaining why someone can't automatically progress to some of our higher-level courses when they have been elsewhere for their introductory courses. It's not because they've not achieved, nor because we are inflexible - it's more often to do with the fact that they have missed vital developmental stages that are necessary for the higher-level assessments.

The plethora of free 'courses' (too often consisting of sitting at a workstation and following a tutorial package) has caused many people to choose their provider on the basis of cost or availability, rather than entering somewhere like our college where an integrated programme is offered in cycles. It's very difficult to tell someone that in preparation for the higher-level exam they now aspire to, they would have been better off being taught in a class here, rather than learning at one of the free centres. It's almost like questioning their judgement – not at all a good way to build a relationship.

How these places have so much money to spend is a mystery – it's almost enough to make you stop taking the local newspaper, as it's so annoying seeing the expensive adverts every week. We spend all of our funding on equipment, training, quality measures and updating our knowledge. Neither our department nor the college as a whole could afford such expensive advertising schemes as those used by the "cherry-picking" companies. We're in the business for the long haul, as part of an integrated programme for everyone, so inevitably our operation will cost more to run. It is a pity so much money is so readily available for the more isolated, limited activities, where often all that is provided is access to a workstation, a guidebook and some help. It may seem fine for many people, but they may not necessarily receive the experienced, strategically planned tuition that our college strives for in a co-ordinated way across the whole curriculum.'

The staff of the college's own IT Learning Centres are quick to deny that the above situation would apply to those following independent programmes under their guidance. 'Our strength comes from being a small unit where we establish a good working relationship with all our learners, whilst remaining within the College. The support we offer is backed by a wealth of experience and dedication provided by qualified staff and this contributes highly to our success,' says Amanda Gordon-Wilson, the IT Centre's manager.

'We have found that the offer of a free course acts as an initial taster to IT and offers new opportunities to people who are otherwise hesitant to try this technology. The portfolio we have on offer gives a flexible alternative for people to learn what they want, when they want, thus allowing their learning to fit in with today's busy lifestyles'. With such a centre as part of the overall college programme, the alternative style is complementary, rather than a competitive alternative.

It is vital that the new open-access opportunities for self-directed study, that have been such a feature of the LSC and the government view of provision, operate within a strategically-planned context. Although highly motivated people can learn quite effectively on their own, there comes a time when expert information, explanation, advice or guidance are necessary for them to make the most of their opportunities.

Many students of all ages have navigated their way through a series of courses and workshops and by doing so built up a substantial portfolio of achievement. 'I am doing the Information Technology courses because they are particularly useful at the moment for me. Before Christmas this year I did the Global Communications course, which involved designing websites. That was really interesting I really enjoyed that, and I have done a Database course, and a presentation and word processing course, and a spreadsheet course.' This student, featured on the College video, then gave a perfect example of the comprehensive curriculum in action: 'Two other courses that I've actually done based at Grey Friars have been the Preliminary Disabled Teachers for Swimming course and the Parent and Child swimming course, and I still work as a swimming teacher on a part-time basis. I can't think of anywhere else that has a variety of courses that are available daytime and evenings'.

With more and better technological advances supporting adult learning, the boundaries of achievement keep extending outwards. But many have pointed out that no matter how exciting and sophisticated IT can be, for the majority of people learning is essentially a social activity – and in adult education everyone learns from each other – including the tutors.

Maths

Numeracy is now one of the Government's target skills and every encouragement is given for adults to follow programmes at all levels. However, there will still be some adult educators in Essex who recall an investigation by Customs and Excise in the 1980s.

Inspectors visited some Essex evening classes in order to form a view on whether adult education class fees should attract VAT. After a visit to a maths class, one inspector reached the conclusion that due to people's varied motivations it is not possible to make a whole-class decision based simply on subject or level. He did feel that those in the GCE 'O' Level maths class who needed the certificate for work purposes such as change of job or promotion within a career were engaged in the class for vocational (therefore serious?) reasons and should not pay VAT.

He had, however, identified a student who told him quite openly that he didn't need the certificate, but "loved maths" and because he was deemed to be gaining pleasure from his (presumably frivolous?) studies, the inspector felt that he should pay VAT on his fee.

Some questions begged to be asked, such as whether the non-VAT payers were still allowed to enjoy their lessons. Or, where the moral justification was in those following the course for, presumably, their individual financial gain being supported by other tax-payers. Subsequently, however, colleagues learned that the idea of differentiated application of VAT was thought to be too complicated to pursue and the threat of more debilitating bureaucracy went away.

In chapter 3, Darien told us of his surprise at 'really enjoying' his maths class and his sense of achievement whilst 'feeling as comfortable as with friends'. Darien appears in the college video as a young 21st Century man bedecked with rings and studs and exactly the kind of person people might assume would say 'It's not for me' where adult education is concerned. Darien and those with similar positive experiences of adult learning should be seen as exemplars – especially for the basic 'school-type' subjects. Grey Friars' motto is, 'It's never too late to learn' and although we often think of older adults in this context, some young adults feel it's too late if they missed out by the time they reach sixteen. The maths department has welcomed many Dariens and even younger people, including, by special arrangement, some 'school-refusers' – and tutors have coaxed and supported them through to achievements they had never thought possible.

They have been joined over the years by hundreds of people in similar situations. Indeed many people have been rescued from the scrap-heap of failed career aspirations by being tutored through to success in mastering maths. Many, with little hope of even understanding, yet alone passing GCE 'O' level (now GCSE) at a satisfactory grade (now a standard requirement for many jobs) owe their twin achievements of improved confidence and new careers to classes at Grey Friars.

Their teacher was most likely to have been Julia Brazear, a long-serving maths tutor who certainly does not subscribe to any hierarchy of motivation, treating her students as individuals, respecting each person's starting point and guiding them in making their own decisions. She is equally happy teaching someone how to work out their change as she is teaching quadratic equations. And yet she never intended to be a teacher: 'I never liked teachers much, I found them generally very bossy control freaks!'

Julia started her working life as an engineer with GEC Marconi, doing research and development. She left to have her two children and in 1979 when the youngest was five, she answered an advertisement to help as a volunteer conversing in English to some Vietnamese 'boat people' who had settled in Colchester. It transpired that they were all talented at maths and Julia undertook some training and started a maths group. She then covered a maths tutor's maternity leave and when the need arose for more maths tutors, she was able to work in both Colchester and Harwich with both adults and in the youth training scheme. At the peak, she was teaching her own classes five mornings per week as well as some work-based training and the maths module of the Access course for mature entrants to higher education.

'I loved teaching adults from the moment I started and I still do – especially when I can change people's feelings about maths. Most of my students have already failed maths at school and my job is to help them see that it really is possible to understand maths. Conquering their fears and mastering the concepts raises people's self-esteem, especially if they gain a qualification.'

Julia is sensitive to her students' feelings. 'They are often very vulnerable and in the small class groups sometimes feel exposed. One student told her husband that she would give the class three weeks - but ended up staying three years! Someone else started in my basic classes and went right through the levels to take a degree in maths and become a teacher.'

She believes a tutor has to be completely prepared for each lesson and should not consider themselves in any way superior to their students just because they know more about maths. 'You have to explain things very clearly and slowly and if that doesn't work you try again in a different way, if necessary three or four times.' If things don't go well, it isn't that the student has failed, it simply means the right way through a barrier hasn't yet been found. 'A person may need a variety of explanations to grasp a difficult concept. If two of us work on it together we outnumber the problem!'

The paperwork isn't an annoyance: 'I've always done my own version anyway and I'm highly organised.' Although when she started Grey Friars felt much 'smaller' as an institution, its growth hasn't affected her feelings about working there. 'Now it is very large, much more structured and highly monitored and better for that. Grey Friars definitely knows where it's at and is ready to provide a proper learning system for everyone. But the ethos is the same and the teaching is the same - as are the students.' But, she says with conviction, 'The college is wickedly under-funded.'

'Teaching at Grey Friars and Harwich has been my life,' Julia says, making light of the fact that she now has to travel by bus as she is no longer allowed to drive. In 1992 she had her eyesight checked and ophthalmic surgeons discovered undetected glaucoma. Operations have left her with 10-degree vision. 'At one time I thought I'd never leave the house again.'

She picked up where she temporarily left off, her enthusiasm undeterred and her effectiveness undiminished. 'I love the Grey Friars building and I have always loved the people I work with. Anyone enthusiastic about teaching should also teach adults. It can be a joy to both teacher and student.'   [AS]

7

Swimming - a Curriculum Model

Grey Friars has developed its educational programmes based upon the concept of a comprehensive curriculum. This requires that, although due regard is given to provision of basic skills as a means of opening the door to further learning, when it comes to designing a curriculum for adults, no subject or level is held to be more important than another. We refer elsewhere to the belief that for a curriculum to be relevant to adult's complex lives it must represent more of a climbing frame than a ladder. People must be enabled to travel in any direction according to their needs at various life stages. Alan Tuckett, the Director of the National Institute of Adult Continuing Education once referred to adults as 'untidy learners.' Grey Friars staff understand what he means, but prefer to view adults as having multiple and changing needs which must be respected. At most staff meetings, principal Alan Skinner can be sure to repeat one of his reminders to tutors: 'Do not forget that there can be as many reasons for attending your course as there are people in the room.'

The current curriculum comprising over 1,000 courses (day, evening, weekend, drop-in and intensive courses) represents not only the national priorities of basic skills and qualification courses, but also represents the interests and needs of local people. Foreign language courses, for example, include at the higher levels both examination classes and non-examined classes. The latter, conducted entirely in the host language may feature geography, social subjects, culture and politics. Arts and crafts include high-level qualifications with City and Guilds as well as beginner and 'taster' classes. Minority crafts, such as paper-making, eggshell decorating, carving, print-making and millinery have been features of the programme which has set out to support traditional crafts by introducing new participants.

New interests are accommodated in the Grey Friars tradition of giving access to all by providing introductory classes, then assisting those who wish to progress – as in the case of Reflexology, where there are now courses for a practitioner's certificate. Additionally, where there is the opportunity for subjects to cross curriculum boundaries, staff enthusiastically embrace collaborative working – for example, in the new applications of IT in subjects such as the languages and art.

In the Grey Friars tradition, there is no need to sub-divide the curriculum except to promote effective teaching and learning and to provide for educational progression.

Swimming, with 113 courses ranging from 13 offered for adult beginners through to teaching certificates can be seen as a paradigm for the whole curriculum.

The programme has been developed to be as open to as many people as possible, with multiple starting points and opportunities for progression not only to higher levels, but also to other aspects of the subject. Also, although Grey Friars concentrates on adult learning, in accordance with its family learning traditions the swimming department offers 24 courses for parents and their children from babies to six years. Emphasis is also placed on swimming for people with a wide range of disabilities. In this sense, due to its inclusive nature, the wide range of subjects and levels and its constantly developing nature, the swimming programme is one of the College's best examples of the comprehensive curriculum in action.

The development of swimming owes everything to a past senior tutor Joan Gurney, who has made it a lifetime's work to get adults into the water. In a teaching career that spanned fifty years, the last thirty were spent in adult education.

Joan Gurney is tall and wears a turquoise track-suit. Her movements are smooth and coordinated; she doesn't look like someone who was born in 1932. As we step inside the building and try to make our way upstairs, Joan is stopped every few metres by a 'Hello, how nice to see you.' I feel like I'm accompanying a TV celebrity. She told me the following anecdote: 'Well, every swimming tutor falls into this trap. I swore I never would. If you meet one of your students, a man perhaps, walking down the street on a sunny afternoon. You greet one another. "Oh, hello, Mrs Gurney." You look but you can't quite recognize him. "Oh, it's Mr Smith. I didn't recognize you with your clothes on."'

Joan, only recently retired although substantially beyond the recognised retirement age, provides us with a graphic picture of specialist curriculum development which counters the often-cited view that adult education programmes were developed in an ad hoc way by well-meaning amateurs. Joan tells the story in her own characteristic way.

'I came to work as a swimming tutor for Grey Friars in 1971/72 when the programme included only two classes. I was not new to the Grey Friars building - in fact I knew every nook and cranny, having been in the Preparatory Department of the Colchester County High School for Girls when it was based here. It was 1938 and I was six years old. I worked my way through the school, leaving from the sixth form in 1951.

I have always had (and still have) a continuous affection and attachment to the building - its past, its imposing architecture, its mystery and its peacefulness amidst the hubbub of the town centre. I was therefore delighted to be made deputy principal in 1974 and renew my association with the building. The principal at that time, appointed in 1973, was the late Enid Bishop. Knowing my background, and being committed to the value of learning to swim, she gave me 'carte blanche' to develop the swimming programme along my own lines with virtually no restrictions attached.

This may have seemed a daunting task, but I had a supportive team of swimming teacher friends. In order to introduce more swimming classes, more water time had to be obtained. Where were the tutors to be found to cover them? A swimming teacher training course was the answer. I already knew that a group of blind and partially sighted people were desperate to obtain some organised, tutored swimming. I also needed more qualified swimming teachers and as the training for this at the time necessitated a residential course at Crystal Palace National Sports Centre, why not set up one in Colchester, I thought?

The programme expanded. By 1979, every type of aquatic activity was catered for - beginners, improvers, parent/child, baby swim, synchronised swimming, aqualung, life saving, swimming for disabled people and Teacher Training (in all disciplines). As new activities (such as aquafit) were introduced by the Amateur Swimming Association (ASA), they were added to the Grey Friars programme.

And then came the first small step in what was to prove a very eventful and action-packed four years. Early in 1979 Colchester Adult Education Centre (as it was then called) became 'recognised' by the ASA.

A Recognised Teaching Centre had to have the facilities for a specified number of regularly staged ASA Training Courses. What an achievement for a centre which did not even have its own pool! Following closely came the Cadbury's Sponsorship Scheme designed to encourage the training of swimming teachers and the encouragement of all age groups (whether disabled or not) to learn to swim. Cadbury's support provided £500. Groups of adults who would not normally have the opportunity to learn to swim were grant-aided, equipment was purchased and a swimming teachers' library (including videos) was established.

In 1980, the Cadbury's grant was renewed for another year and nominations were requested for people who made outstanding progress under the scheme. ASA and Cadbury's marked the success of the scheme; Mr Andrew Millar and the late Mrs Joan Hilliard (both blind) were among six people from the whole country honoured for their achievements. They were mentioned in the local and national press and appeared on national television. Grey Friars received congratulatory letters from the County Education Officers and the Inspector for Physical Education. In June, two of our swimming tutors, Wyn Robinson and the late Win Duane, received long service awards from the Royal Life Saving Society, presented at a ceremony in Liverpool by Prince Michael of Kent.

In August, an ambitious National Swimming Teachers' Summer School was held at the University of Essex. Students came from as far as Wales, the Isle of Wight and Germany. Three pools were needed to train Teachers of Disabled People, Diving and Synchronised Swimming. In November another tutor, the late Freda Starkey, was elected National President of the Swimming Teachers' Association, and the late Win Duane received the Henry Pike Memorial Shield for services to swimming in 1980.

To round off the year, Andrew Millar (who was not only a good swimmer, but also a keen tape recordist) made a complete record of the Cadbury's celebration with David Wilkie, entered some of his tapes in the British Amateur Tape Recordists' Contest and swept the board. He took the ACOS Cup for his interview with David. In addition, he took the cup for the "Best Overall Tape" and the cup for the best entry from a disabled person.

What a year 1980 had been! Nevertheless 1981 turned out to be just as remarkable as the previous one. Cadbury's sponsorship was renewed for a final year. In April a Sports Injuries Conference was organised jointly with the University.

At a special ceremony in 1980 Joan and Andrew swim with Olympic Gold Medallist, David Wilkie.

1981 was the International Year of the Disabled. There was more publicity for us because of our exceptional provision of Swimming for Disabled People. Five of our tutors were specially selected by the ASA / Cadbury Scheme to receive an intensive training course over one week at Crystal Palace. I was one of them. Immediately after this, plans were made for a class especially for those who had been advised by their doctors to swim for the benefit of their health. This class was called 'Swim Back to Health'. It was given good publicity in the local press and 20 adults eventually enrolled to receive specialist tuition.

At this point disaster struck and were it not for the persistence of a courageous team of tutors it would have been the final curtain for this extensive swimming programme built up over many years. Essex County Council Education Committee decided to close 24 indoor school swimming pools over the winter months in order to make a saving of £300,000. Not only did we write letters to MPs, protest, campaign, organise petitions and generally make our voices heard, but we also systematically set about finding alternative facilities to tide them over the crisis. Lexden Springs Special School in Colchester agreed to accommodate classes. The Garrison authorities extended their hours. Two classes of life savers moved to a privately owned pool. Swimming teacher training courses were re-scheduled. Nothing, in fact, was lost, and if anything the number of classes increased.

In November, Andrew Millar, the Centre's most famous blind student, repeated his success of the previous year in the National Tape Recordists' Annual Contest. I was chosen by swimming teachers from across Great Britain as the recipient of the Swimming Teacher's Association Henry Pike Memorial Trophy for outstanding services to swimming in 1981, but, once again, Andrew Millar had the final word – very significantly in this International Year of Disabled People. In the closing week of 1981, he was awarded Colchester Sports Council's Trophy 'Sport for All' in recognition of his long and varied association with a myriad of exciting sports.

1982 opened with renewed attempts to persuade Essex County Council to re-open the 25 indoor school pools. In March, Andrew Millar was presented with his Eastern Region Service to Sport Award by sports commentator, Ron Pickering. We heard once more that, as an ASA Recognised Teaching Centre, sponsorship had been granted, this time by Sun Life Assurance in their special Adult Learn to Swim Campaign - £1.00 for every adult who learned to swim at least 10 metres in the course of the year. A short piece written for the local press brought in a huge response. By the end of June, 58 adult beginners had gained their 10 metre certificates and 132 adults had learned to swim in 9 months. This total exceeded every centre in the country and another presentation of honours came our way.

Once again, we featured in the Royal Life Saving Society's National Honours List for the year - in June Wyn Robinson received the Recognition Badge and the late Mr Ken Herbert the President's Commendation of the Society. In June also came the news that Essex County Council's Education Committee was considering ways of keeping the 25 school pools open over the winter months of 1983/84. 'Colchester Sports Centre announced that it was to take part in the launch of the National Sports Council's 50+ 'In the Swim' campaign and at the invitation, 150 people from Grey Friars (including disabled swimmers) immediately volunteered to participate, demonstrate, swim, teach – anything aquatic from complete beginners to synchronised swimming.

Once more, the year had a grand finale. In December, Essex County Council agreed to re-introduce all-year heating for the 25 school pools which would re-open in April 1983. There is no doubt that the activity and protests generated by our dedicated team played a large part in this dramatic discussion, and it was a fitting tribute to their determination and perseverance.

By 1983, our outstanding swimming achievements were known country-wide. I attended many national conferences that year and was always greeted with "Oh, you're from the centre that does all those marvellous things in swimming". But the emphasis this year was on the Government Sponsored 'Look After Yourself' scheme and the National Sports Council's '50+ All to Play For' campaign, both of which included swimming. Eight potential 'Look After Yourself' tutors were grant-aided for national training and, together with the 50+ campaign, generated more press coverage. A one day Seminar and Workshop on 'Popmobility' was held in association with the University of Essex.

Joan Gurney, left, receives an award on behalf of Grey Friars.

Yet again, Grey Friars came out top in the Sun Life Adult Learn to Swim Campaign, clocking up more adults who had mastered the skill than anywhere else in the country (including Crystal Palace National Sports Centre).

I always felt that there was something bigger to come and that all this swimming activity was like a sleeping volcano ready to erupt in to something gigantic. And then it came! The Eastern Region of the Sports Council announced that we had won a special trophy for the most outstanding organisational contribution to sport. It was awarded for exceptional activities in all aspects of swimming for adults, including the training of teachers and swimming for disabled students. The judges acknowledged at the same time that we had managed a wide range of other sports for all levels of ability.

At the peak of this success there were between 150 and 200 varied classes per year and thirty swimming tutors in the team. Every one of them I remember with gratitude and affection. Memories of students flood back - their support and fortitude in the bad as well at the good times. They were all dedicated people, not statistics.' A full version of Joan's reminiscences plus an archive of cuttings and photographs, is in preparation, and her Girls' High School memories are available in a booklet available from Grey Friars.

As for paperwork, Joan says that it isn't easy to fill in forms in a wet bathing suit by the side of the pool. The tutors get frustrated.

'Asking a dripping wet parent with a dripping wet young child to fill in a form and tick boxes is not the easiest task. They don't carry a pen. If they wear a hearing aid it isn't in. It is incredibly difficult. The tutors struggle.'

I know that the Learning and Skills Council want the evidence that we are doing the right thing and that everyone is qualified and doing the right work in order to get our funding, but I really think that it goes over the top.'

Joan sums up: 'The purpose is sound; the practice is tedious. These systems, she says, are set up by 'someone who has certainly never taught swimming.'

We agree that you do not need many inspections to evaluate a tutor's work. If the numbers keep up in a class and people succeed in their learning then the tutor is working satisfactorily. There is no better judge of a tutor's performance than the fee-paying student.

Is adult education in a healthy state?

Joan says, 'From the point of view of the student it is pretty healthy. People take more holidays abroad hence the continuing interest in languages. Emphasis on health and fitness increases.' But Joan complains about the 'Nanny state, interfering too much in certain matters I believe are personal.'

What are her thoughts on non-accredited classes struggling for funding in future years? 'Students come for all sorts of reasons: they want a fulfilling evening out in the company of friends. I don't look behind reasons too much; people make all sorts of choices. The accredited courses will be all right. But people also want relaxation and confidence and they don't always want a qualification at the end. Swimming, although a jewel in the crown, is only one jewel among many.'

Joan is right, of course, that enjoyment is a basic foundation for adult education and we should not forget this in the drive for qualifications, qualifications, qualifications.   [DS]

8

Learning for its Own Sake

The previous chapter showed how the swimming department has a comprehensive subject offer within a comprehensive curriculum. The same can apply to other departments. Health and Fitness has a popular range of courses from beginner to professional level. Many new courses include holistic therapies, meditation, visualisation, Egyptian ('belly') dance and Argentine tango. Baby massage courses are popular with parents, not only for their therapeutic physical effects, but also for the empathy they can bring.

Aikido

Maurice Sheenan started practising aikido in the early eighties; his wife Eileen went along to see what he was up to and became equally hooked. They have been teaching at the Wilson Marriage Centre for ten years. 'It seems magical doesn't it,' said Maurice as we watched his wife gently throw a larger male to the floor using techniques of balance rather than brute strength. The students all know how to fall without hurting themselves.

Aikido is a comparatively 'new' martial art. As a sport it began in Japan in the 1930s; its moves are based on Jujitsu, and on Japanese sword fighting. Maurice believes Aikido - the way of harmony - takes the best of many martial arts. 'But it doesn't seek to inflict pain,' he says. He and Eileen wear the traditional white canvas cotton pyjama suit, but due to their elevated rank as 4th Dan black belts they wear a black pleated cotton skirt as well. It gives their movements much grace as the pleats swing around their legs.

At first it seemed strange to me to watch a group of westerners wearing Japanese pyjamas and bowing to one another before they execute a movement. The tutors use the correct Japanese terms for the exercise mat and the various exercises that are taught in sequence.

Maurice believes that the practice of aikido, which will improve posture and general fitness, confers other benefits - you learn not to be intimidated. Maurice and Eileen are both in their sixties but Aikido keeps them looking much younger. There is no typical aikido student. Ages range from twenties to sixties although one regular member is in his seventies. Maurice tells me that the founder of aikido himself was still practising until his death, aged eighty-nine.

Tara was one of the beginners for this term's sessions, a bright-eyed seventeen year old studying for an International Baccalaureate at the Institute. So she was not wearing the white pyjamas. Her aikido class will count toward her final grade. And she fully intends to continue the practice when she starts university. 'I like the way it's about inner not outer strength' she says.

She was being partnered in the exercise by Justin who after six years has achieved his black belt. So, like the tutors, he was wearing the skirt. He started simply as a means of helping a dodgy knee and found the practice cured the knee and he was hooked. He refers to aikido as one of the softer martial arts.' It keeps the energy flow going; it balances you out.' Now that he has achieved black belt status he will work toward the Dan grades and it will take him one to three years.

While the session is under way, strong discipline is in evidence. Maurice demonstrated this to me by clapping his hands. The mat fell silent; each person stopped what they were doing. 'This discipline is essential. It is both a safety measure and also shows respect to the sensei, the teacher. It's for safety but also for dignity and respect.' Justin said, 'I don't find the discipline overpowering.'

In a side room six more advanced students accompanied Maurice to practise moves fighting with swords (in this case special wooden sticks). As the wooden sword fighting continues - a practice of six stylised moves - you can sense the exhilaration of the six participants, who are striking and whirling their batons in unison.

Is there any danger in the sport?

Maurice laughed. 'It's remarkably accident free. I like to think that it is because we are so careful.'

Do he and Eileen ever disagree over teaching?

'Of course not. It's like handwriting. The letters are the same, but the shape is different. Each one teaches in their own manner. We do not let husband and wife partner one another though.' He didn't elaborate.

The session ends with a cool down exercise. The participants bow, leave the mat and put on their sandals. An air of quiet dignity prevails. Maurice and Eileen appreciate the use of the main hall at Wilson Marriage to stand in for a dogon. Do they have a wish list? 'I suppose showers and changing rooms,' says Maurice, 'but we are very happy with the hall.'

Twice a year a chief examiner, who lives in America, comes and tests the students to see whether they are ready to move up a grade. As one student said, 'I am intrigued by a technique that allows you to overcome strength by guile and training.'   [DS]

The Summer School programme started small and is now another jewel in the Grey Friars crown. In the twenty-fifth year, 184 courses were offered. The number of students in June 2004 was 1,554.

The Summer Schools give tutors the chance to offer some offbeat subjects and the summer 'fourth leg' of the academic year can also offer taster subjects. You can for example spend a day studying papier-mache techniques. Or why not brush up on your Salsa and Merengue dancing on a June evening or spend an evening learning the Argentine Tango? Most of the departments at Grey Friars run short summer school courses and they are often unique to an adult education college. Where else could you learn in a day how to make embroidered cards to keep or in two evening classes master e-mail for beginners and then go on to a day's intensive course – followed by an office-related workshop using computers? If you enjoyed your short art course in watercolours or some other technique, who knows what other art course you may apply for next September. Short, practical introductory sessions in foreign languages could whet the appetite for more study in September, for interest or for exams.

The Summer School also provides an opportunity to offer the sort of courses that could be described as life-affirming. Fledgling confidence can grow after some sessions with Colin Kirby-Green called Drawing for the Terrified. His colleague Keith Whitelock offers Watercolours for the Terrified. For three days of four hours a day, you will have the chance to bring back to life talent that has been buried under the normal hurly-burly of a busy life.

Another important aspect of the summer school is the emphasis on providing courses for adults with learning difficulties and disabilities also Skills for Life activities. There are nearly fifty free courses in this section of the programme. Because Summer School courses are so short there is seldom the problem of student drop out.

What are summer school courses like? Here is a snapshot of Keith Whitelock's three-day summer school course. It's an early afternoon in late July. We've travelled from Grey Friars to Layer Marney, the eight-storey Tudor gatehouse some miles to the south west. We're at the top of the high tower, up among the tall twisting red-brick chimneys, and when you look down you can see the grounds pooling into an oasis of green lapped by the brown of ripe wheat fields. It's an oasis that at the moment is spotted with artists and their easels, all utterly absorbed in responding to the beauty of the place, and representing it in line and colour.

Pigeons coo. White butterflies flit hither and thither. The breeze rustles the trees. Keith is busy moving from student to student, talking to them one-to-one. He offers encouragement, discussing ways in which work can be improved. 'That's nice,' he'll say, pointing to part of a painting, 'but this is excellent.' Sometimes he suggests a different approach to a subject, perhaps focusing on an object close up rather than attempting a general view.

Everyone seems so relaxed that it would be easy to assume there's no learning going on. But once you start talking to tutor and students, as I did on the final day of the course, you soon realise that themes that have come up time and time again in this book are being repeated here.

Adult education, which quietly and unquestioningly welcomes and accepts the varied academic and emotional experience of adults, has the power to enrich and strengthen them, and to help them move on in their lives. It is a token of a sane, caring and enabling society.

Keith Whitelock

Keith, the tutor, used to work in shops in Colchester, and then started going to art classes at Grey Friars. He did a Link course, designed to prepare students for degree-level study and an art foundation course, then went on to take a degree in illustration at Wolverhampton. Because he had enjoyed Grey Friars so much as a student, he came back to be a tutor here, combining that with freelance work. He is keen on Grey Friars because it combines a very good range of courses with a high level of tutoring. His particular concern is the keeping open of satellite venues, to bring courses to the surrounding villages for people who can't easily get into Colchester. Maybe they don't have cars, maybe their physical mobility is limited, maybe travelling into town costs too much. Keith feels it's very important that these people should have access both to education and to the social contact that goes with it.

Most of the students here are veterans of art courses. There's just one who is new. Helen, a working mum in her thirties, loved art at school, but hasn't done any since. Adult education isn't new to her, though; she did her accountancy training as an adult. She's on maternity leave at the moment; her partner has taken time off to look after their ten-week-old baby so she can do this course. She's enjoying it very much, and hopes to go on to do an evening course at Grey Friars. She has spent the last three days drawing, doing experiments in tone.

Ron is also on this course to experiment. An ex-tailor, ex-London-cabdriver, he's very experienced with oils, loves going to exhibitions and reading the biographies of artists. At one point he was thinking of doing a degree in Fine Art, but the amount of study that he had to put into acquiring The Knowledge to qualify for his taxi licence discouraged him; he didn't want to undertake anything that required such a high level of commitment again. So adult education suits him fine. He's now trying watercolours for the first time: his skill at drawing and his observation of light are apparent. He's caught the complex windows of the tower beautifully, and on this sunny afternoon he is busy adding shadows that weren't there earlier in the week. At the tutor's suggestion he has also happily painted a close-up of an urn, to help him get the feel of watercolours, and develop his skills. He's found this course extremely useful.

The amount of work done by each student over the three days varies. One student has concentrated on a single watercolour painting, leaving blank until the last moment the foreground of vibrant flowers. She's been coming to classes for about twelve years. She understands how watercolour works. 'Things click and you know what you're doing,' she explains. She's obviously a perfectionist. Quite quiet. And then suddenly she's explaining how much adult education means to her; how she suffered from depression for years following her husband's suicide that left her to care for their five children alone, how her world has opened out since she started coming to classes. 'I was shaking and shivering the first time I went into Grey Friars,' she remembers. But she loved the courses and the social contact that came with them, felt alive again, has tried new things, like pottery. 'There are other reasons than education for adult ed,' she says wryly. 'It saves the health service money.'

Grey Friars courses have also been therapeutic for eighty-two year old William, a war-disabled ex-school-caretaker, a widower. 'I started doing painting when I retired,' he says. 'Have you enjoyed this course?' I ask him. 'Oh my golly yes,' he says. 'I feel privileged at my age to have this kind of quality,' he says. 'I paint and draw. I enjoy it... The old armchair can wait.' Sadly he has, as he puts it, 'resigned' from Grey Friars now. He loves the art room in the old building, and the camaraderie of the classes, but he can't any longer face climbing to room 25 with all his art materials.

One determined student has sat resolutely for three days in front of what seems to be a disused fountain, making profile and full-face studies of the mossy carved heads with their stoppered mouths which remind her of the Green Man, using colour washes to convey shape and shadow. Behind her a live fountain tinkles, cooling the warm air. Sandals crunch on the gravel path, bees buzz on spikes of lavender. But she is intent, concentrating, dedicated. So much so that in term-time she went to three different art classes. She appreciates what she calls the 'combined consciousness' of people working together.

Maybe that's part of the reason another student has come with her friend. They started art classes together in Mersea when they retired, needing each other's moral support – though her greatest fan is her nine-year-old grandson who invariably says, 'Gran, that's lovely!' when she shows him her work. She's appreciated this course: 'I have learnt a lot from it,' she says. 'Keith's a very good tutor.' And she enjoys the atmosphere of adult education: 'Although you're learning, it's not starchy.'

Almost every student's story links back to Grey Friars in some way: the old building is a vivid presence in their lives. Take Janet, who was at school here from when she was five, in the days when there was strict uniform, a gymslip and white shirt, blazer and panama hat, with underwear of liberty bodice and navy blue knickers. Her classroom was where the reception area now is. They had meals with raw cabbage, sago and tapioca pudding. Sometimes they did art outside in an arbour. The drawback for her, as it is for William, is the lack of lift, and having to carry her art materials up the stairs to the art room. She has been painting for four years, and likes the detail of painting architecture. She has found this course and its location inspiring.

In the last half hour of the day the class assembles in the long gallery under the beady glass eyes of a stuffed stag's head, the sun falling slantwise through the tall windows on the polished floor. The students balance their paintings on the panelling, prop them at the foot of the wall. Where necessary, Keith uses masking tape to hold them up. 'It's been three lovely days,' he says, and remarks on the 'diverse range of response to this wonderful place', for example pure watercolour, pencil, watercolour with charcoal and watercolour with pastels. He goes through every student's work in front of the group, picking out the strengths of each piece and commenting. He suggests that where paintings aren't completed, students should return to finish them; and that perhaps they might like to exchange phone numbers so that they can come back in twos and threes rather than alone.

And then the class splits up. Some students carry their paintings and easels out to their cars, others stay on, concentrating once more on their work. A black and white spaniel sidles through the open tower door. Sheep bleat. It's a timeless scene. And what's impressed me most is the importance that adult education has in students' lives.   [MF]

Summer Music School

The hall at Grey Friars - a lofty room with 14 clerestory windows and a dais with a boudoir grand piano. It's a room that fulfils a variety of functions ranging from meetings to exhibitions to Scottish dancing, It is July 16th and Bill Tamblyn is giving the final session of a three week summer school, Gospel and African Song Workshop, a short course of three workshops spread over three weekday mornings for two hours. Bill took his group of twenty through the music and the movement leading by example.

The quality of tutors at Grey Friars can be outstanding. They do not teach for the high salaries, but they teach because they adore their subjects and wish to share their knowledge with other adults. Bill Tamblyn or rather Professor William Tamblyn has for years headed the music school at Colchester Institute. Recently retired he has begun to offer courses like the one in this summer school. To have a tutor of Bill's quality is made possible by the part time nature of much adult education teaching. Because he is retired he is able to offer these courses. Thus it happens that a beginner singer can be tutored by someone of national status.

At the final session the group performed the repertoire they had studied. The small audience was composed of friends and partners. To be a spectator was to see music being made by a mixed group of people, mostly women. Their ages ranged from the twenties upwards. Some of the songs were accompanied with African skin drums, others the piano. Bill had imported one of the Colchester Institute students, a brilliant young pianist. Other songs were *a cappella*. He conducted his amateurs with as much vigour as if he were conducting the national Philharmonic.

His audacious choice of songs, instead of intimidating the amateur performers, challenged them. One song sung in the original Shona language was an anti-apartheid song. Between the songs, Bill gave the audience a running commentary on the music. He pointed out that Elvis Presley had started out as a Gospel singer. "Elvis sang as a white man in the style of a black man."

The group stood in a semi circle on the parquet floor of the hall with Bill in the middle facing them, and sang. They were not as rhythmic as a genuine black gospel choir but they still had the small audience clapping along with them. It made an impressive sight watching a dozen and a half Colchestrians singing a Negro spiritual as though they meant it. Unaccompanied, they sang Jesus travels around the world.

After a few songs, Bill got his whole class to dance with the beat and he joined in. It was all most un-English. Of course, Tamblyn is an impresario and like all choir masters he has the charisma to make the choir follow him. In a choir, like an orchestra, the parts combine into something larger than the sum of the components. Most of the singers were beginners, a few had done a singing course before, and one was a professional actress.

"It was demanding for beginners," one of the women told me. "He pushed us, but it was good fun."

As I left the hall at lunch-time the session was over but an impromptu group was forming around the pianist. Bill has been engaged to run music courses for Grey Friars for the new academic year 2004/5.   [DS]

The Summer School attracts interest from far and wide. A profile of the college in a national adult education journal included a snippet of college life and a photograph of a middle-aged lady and her bike in front of Grey Friars, looking just as if she had cycled from the other side of town – not so! She turned out to be a student who had earlier surprised staff with a telephone call from Rotterdam to check if all was well with the 3-day patchwork course. Meike van Floudt was about to set off on her bicycle to catch the ferry to Harwich.

On another occasion, a fax arrived from Japan asking for an urgent fax-back of the full prospectus, followed by a request for some Summer School outlines for a professor from Keio University, Tokyo, who was coming to England.

A fax and credit card enrolment from Mrs van der Watt from Reitz, South Africa caused a stir in the office when she contacted Grey Friars to enrol for some art courses.

And notable addresses appearing in the mailing list recently included Denmark, Alicante and two from Inverness, rendering others such as Berkshire and Oxfordshire comparatively local!

Creative Writing

Dorothy Schwarz writes: When I came home from living in France with my foreign correspondent husband and five children, part-time teaching seemed a worthwhile alternative to being a full time Mum. As a published but not well-known writer and with a degree but no teacher training, I offered my skills to Grey Friars. They already had a creative writing tutor - a teacher from the Sixth Form College, but offered me a slot at Grey Friars. I took my first class in the autumn of 1984 an 'absolute beginner'. From the first week I was drawn in to the Grey Friars ethos - enthusiasm and helpfulness from the management and clerical staff, part of the friendly atmosphere as soon as you enter the building.

Senior staff in the 1980s were also under less external pressure and were much more able to establish their own priorities. You could have coffee or share a sandwich with Alan Skinner the principal, or Diana McLeod the vice principal, or Howard Leyshon the longest-serving senior member of staff. They were interested to hear about the work from different perspectives and were always open to new ideas and suggestions for improvement. Unlike a college with a majority of full-time staff however, you had less contact with your tutor colleagues, because we would mostly come in for our class and then leave. As a tutor, you were expected to keep up to date records of students and their work. You were expected to produce lesson plans, schemes of work and syllabuses, but how you did it was up to you. There was no set formula, nor particular framework to which you had to adhere. As a way of working it suited my temperament. Teaching one or two classes a week gave me enough time for my maternal and household duties and for my own writing.

Creative Writing as a subject lies completely within the non-accredited sphere. When I started in the 1980s it was not taught at university level. Now in the first decade of the twenty-first century it has become a respectable part of many university programmes at degree and post-graduate level. And qualifications can now be gained in the subject.

Some students have come to my courses convinced that they only have to scribble down their experiences and an eager publishing house will buy the manuscript and turn it into a best seller. Sadly, not true. In the twenty years or so I have taught Creative Writing it has grown harder not easier to publish and there are more and more eager aspirants for every publishing slot. I cannot promise any student that their work will become a best seller or any sort of seller at all. What I can promise is that if a student completes a course of six or ten or twelve or twenty sessions, his or her writing will improve in fluency. The ultimate aim of my creative writing course is to enable the student to find his or her own authentic writing voice. Whether or not that voice will turn out to become marketable depends on other issues.

A cross section of our local community enrols in creative writing courses. There can be a proportion of dropouts. There are those who think that it was going to be easy and then find writing is a craft that needs far more practice than they imagined, or, they may find they simply cannot keep up a regular attendance. A student may have problems at work, in their personal life or something as simple as an unreliable child minder. But in my course, as in the others at Grey Friars, a group dynamic normally develops between the students and the tutor and amongst the students themselves and this can be very supportive.

It requires far more effort to follow an evening course when you are an adult with adult duties and responsibilities compared to being a school age or a college student when all you are supposed to do is study. (Of course this applies less to college students nowadays who are also forced to work now that grants are so much reduced or in some cases non-existent.) Tutors who teach adults are always pleased at the high motivation their students display. For myself, watching the progress a writer makes from those first fumbling efforts towards producing a readable and entertaining piece of writing never fails to thrill. As much now after teaching more than fifty courses, the thrill does not diminish for me.

I base my course on the theory and practice of the short story, although many students are writing or have the intention to write a novel. I take the short story as a form because once you can write a good short story, you can tackle a novel. Students come to creative writing with a multiplicity of motives. Common to nearly all however, is the desire (whether or not admitted) to see work in print. I will try and guide the students towards suitable avenues for publication. Sadly there are few and the number decreases as small press publications are forced out in a competitive market.

One increasing field however is the short story competition. When I started there were only a few annually, so we developed our own. For three years in the early 1990s, a good response produced anthologies. 'My World, Your World' included work judged by Andrew Motion, Ronald Blythe and Jonathan Gash. 'The Anthology' in 1991 was judged by Herbert Lomas, Ruth Rendell and Lindsay Clarke. 'Write On – Read On' in 1995, was our third publication and we chose to operate this as a co-operative editorial effort between the three Grey Friars creative writing classes. Now there are literally hundreds - writing circles, BBC, universities, magazines all offer competitions from the narrowly local to national and international. I encourage students to submit their work

Success however doesn't necessarily have to be judged by external criteria like publication. In a dynamic creative writing class I don't believe what the tutor expounds provides the core experience. No, in a creative writing class, what is important is that the students read their own work aloud, submitting it to analysis and comment from the group thus providing an exciting and solid learning experience. We take turns to comment one after another and it is always revealing to see who likes what and whether there is a consensus about the piece. This can be a stimulating, exciting and illuminating experience.

Tutor training

Although all staff had always been encouraged to undertake qualifications, or at the least to attend the in-service support programme, tutors of non-accredited courses were now directly being asked to do teacher training.

This was in line with increased insistence on paper qualifications from government. Although I had a degree in history, I had never done a Cert. Ed. (Certificate in Education). In conformity with new regulations, I had to complete the City and Guilds Teaching Certificate, parts one and two. Grey Friars provided the venue and for their unqualified tutors the courses were free. I recall grumbling together with a swimming tutor of many years' experience about why we had to jump through hoops. But at the end of the second course we ate our words. The course material provided little that we did not already practise, but what it did was to systematise our practices and show us the theory behind good practice. To think through what are your aims and objectives for any learning experience can only be strengthening.

Further Developments from Classes

Positive spin-offs from classes at Grey Friars are many and various. Several are described in this book. Because the atmosphere at Grey Friars is so conducive to activity, many classes do contain spin-offs, some spontaneous, others planned into the scheme of work.

I'd like to describe three spin-offs from Creative Writing: the email list, student follow-ons and publishing a book of our work.

Since the growth of the internet many students have access to computers. In several of my classes we have compiled an email list of students. On this list any member can post a story for general comment. I can also post notices of literary events, competitions or calls for submissions from magazines. There are three of these lists available at the time of writing.

When a class ends after 6, 10 or 12 weeks, some of the students choose to go on meeting. They may meet monthly or weekly in a pub or someone's home. It provides continuity and they enjoy this. One of my groups, 'Innovations' in 2000 contained a group of keen writers. We often discussed the problems of getting published. Students would bring in their work and we would read pieces that everyone enjoyed but, in the present competitive commercial market, it was hard to see how they would publish and where. The idea of producing a book arose spontaneously. No one put up the idea first; it simply arrived and like Topsy 'it growed and growed'.

Our idea was to ask for submissions of poetry, prose and short stories from Colchester and the surrounding districts. We would then have a selection committee who would choose which pieces to put into the anthology. Five of us volunteered to read entries and we were off.

We applied for grants from Colchester Borough Council and Essex County Council and were given £2000. Provided that the editors worked for free, printing a small book would be a viable proposition. Gerald Ferguson, one of the editorial team, agreed to sell some adverts. Paul Cathmoir, a fine amateur poet, agreed to winnow out the poetry submissions. Finally after six month's work, meeting most fortnights in one or other of our houses we were ready to publish 'Homegrown'. There were some polished submissions from local writers like Heather Reyes and Frank Dullaghan. Some of the pieces chosen were from writers who had been published already, but at least half were from first timers. Paul's dad, a professional photographer, gave us our cover photo free of charge. The book was sold for £2.50 with proceeds to go to the Grey Friars Lift Fund.

The College and the Borough Council's Arts Department helped us fund a launch party. Several of the authors read their pieces to a well-filled hall of contributors and their friends at Grey Friars. It was such a genuinely co-operative effort.

For me the best moment was indubitably when Mathew Chapman read his poem 'To a very small ant'.

You fell from the sweet honey of my plum tree
into the harsh synthetics of my car.
So tiny, no bigger than three letters in four-point type,
you sit upon my thumbnail,
perfect antennae seeking, seeking.
Separated now from your myriad sisters
you shall not regain your tumultuous city,
not caress comrade, nor worship Divine Mother:
There is nothing now but search in barren desert – shall I
kill you with swift blow or crushing slide of thumb
and end your search, your sorrow?
I snap my thumb: you fall into the carpet.

Perhaps in God's mercy
some crevice of it may seem
for a precious moment
the labyrinthine ways
of Home.

Mathew kept his overcoat on, although the hall was warm. It was his first reading in public and his first published poem. He was eighty years old.

In the hall, published and known writers mingled with the unknown; everyone felt a sense of achievement. This is the great advantage of non-accredited courses; they are open-ended.

[DS]

Sue Robbins

Sue is another tutor of a non-accredited course, teaching English Literature. This is her story. She writes: 'Although I managed somehow to get through a few G.C.E. 'O' levels at school I failed my maths with an atrocious grade. Many years later, that stigma of failure was still part of my psyche and in a sudden burst of bravado I enrolled at Grey Friars for an evening course in that dreaded subject. To my utter amazement, this time around I passed with an unbelievable 'A' grade.

This achievement, which I deem nothing short of miraculous, whetted my appetite and I became a Grey Friars groupie taking evening classes in 'O' level French, 'A' level English and 'A' level History. Having been a book-worm all my life and passionate about all types of literature I then went on to study for my B.A. in English and History. Although I completed this degree for personal development, a friend told me about a meeting at Grey Friars for people who might be interested in teaching adults. I was intrigued. I went along, got hooked and enrolled right away for my Further Education Teaching Certificate. So here I am back again, but this time in front of the learners rather than being one of them.

If someone had told me I would become a tutor in the building where I battled with percentages, proportions and probability – which I'm sure I still don't fully understand - my response would have been one of incredulity and amazement - but here I am as a tutor of literature running 10 week non-accredited courses and I could not be happier.

My first attempt however at this new venture was, to say the least, a little shaky. Full of enthusiasm and eager to make my mark on further education I spent the summer of 2002 designing my first course which I called Shakespeare's World of Tragedy and Comedy. I chose *King Lear* and *Much Ado About Nothing* to reflect these two genres. I designed posters and leaflets and displayed them wherever I could and was geared up for an influx of devoted followers of Shakespeare for my September evening class. Oh dear, reality dawned - the register showed four enrolments! Undeterred I hired a room and decided to run the course privately. Those wonderfully encouraging folk who came supported me in my next evening course which I ran, through Grey Friars, the following January and this time with a full complement of learners keen to be introduced to American literature. Everyone enjoyed it and came back for more! I continued with the classic theme and ran more 10-week evening courses on some of the best English novels, including George Orwell's *1984*, Aldous Huxley's *Brave New World*, Virginia Woolf's *To the Lighthouse*, Emily Brontë's *Wuthering Heights* and Mary Shelley's *Frankenstein*.

These courses have been a joy to run, as there is such diversity in the learners' ages and life experiences and this really stimulates discussion. I have career men and women, those who are taking time out from work and retired folk. No one is excluded. It is important to acknowledge a learner's contribution and give praise and continued encouragement to them. If this had happened to me when I took that dreaded 'O' level Maths exam I may have scraped through because I will never forget what my maths teacher told me after the results came through: 'I thought you would have passed that without any trouble.' Some of you may be familiar with lack of encouragement. If my teacher had only given me that support at the time, who knows what heights I might have climbed!

It is so important to acknowledge everyone's effort and recognise that all opinions are valid and should be treated with respect - whether from a learner who is familiar with the material or from someone who is experiencing the work for the first time and needs support.

Support is a two-way relationship and I've had the pleasure of welcoming back each term those who supported me from the beginning of my teaching career and new folk who join them, including some Chinese and Japanese students. I have experienced the learners coming together through sharing their love of literature and being free to express their own opinions in an informal environment.

This relaxed atmosphere forms an important feature of a non-accredited course - there is less external pressure on the learners. If one theme engages them, I can if necessary, allow this to continue longer than I had planned.

However, it is vital to have a structured and properly planned course. Design and planning take a very long time! I start researching for my new courses whilst I am running the current ones. I discover as much as I can about my chosen subject and start to work out a schedule and syllabus. I select themes which I think will be interesting and stimulating and arrange them into ten 2-hour slots. I create diversity in the class with a mixture of presentations, informal discussion, group work, 'fun' quizzes, text reading and video clips.

Flexibility and versatility are major factors which attract those learners who do not want the strict regime of coursework, homework and the pressure of an examination, but who still want the opportunity to share thoughts and opinions with others of a like mind. I have found my students enthusiastic, open minded and insightful and I admire them when they battle against the elements on a cold winter's night to come to class. Above all, they are highly self-motivated. On these non-accredited courses the students study for its own sake which is the best form of motivation. There is no material reward at the end – no external piece of paper to prove success. Their achievement is the pleasure and satisfaction it brings and the internal factor of enhancing personal development. They enrol because they want to, not because they have to.

Because of this honest desire to learn, I feel so privileged to be their tutor. They all come initially not knowing who I am, what their experiences will be, whether they will enjoy the commitment they have made - and what is more they have actually paid to be there. I feel it is imperative to preserve this form of further education for everyone - at a cost which is affordable. From being a student to having the privilege of becoming a tutor has opened up a whole new life of challenges and opportunities. I passionately hope that the availability of these non-accredited courses will not diminish - as they entertain, empower and educate not only the learners, but also the tutors. The profile of this non-exam part of the adult curriculum must be raised to ensure it remains a positive trademark of Grey Friars' history as an Adult Community College.'

9

The Value of Adult Learning

Learning often has an effect on students' lives far beyond the classroom. Students gain in confidence; learning can help in coping with disability and to bridge gaps between generations.

The Wider Benefits of Lifelong Learning Research Centre, a government-funded joint initiative between Birkbeck College and the Institute of Education at the University of London, is setting out to quantify and assess the effects of learning above and beyond meeting government targets and the demands of the economy. It researches benefits to individuals at personal and community level; the ways in which learning may affect health, ageing, citizenship, crime and parenting, for example. These are more complex and subtle. Certainly they are not reducible to a statistic such as the number of examination passes. Findings are being published in a series of papers, presentations and books.[1]

Benefits of adult education beyond gains in economic and academic achievement have been addressed by official reports in the past. The opening statement of the Russell Report of 1972 [2] concludes 'The value of education is not solely to be measured by direct increases in earning power or productive capacity or by any other materialistic yardstick, but by the quality of life it inspires in the individual and generates for the community at large.' Russell's recommendations dealt with the need for advisory bodies, co-operative planning, local authority direct provision of a wide curriculum, residential educational opportunities for adults and, in relation to educational building programmes, to 'take into account the particular needs of adult education.'

Grey Friars operates in a way that reflects many of the recommendations in the Russell Report, and also exemplifies some of what QC Helena Kennedy argues for in *Learning Works*, the report from her 1997 'Widening Participation Committee' of the Further Education Funding Council.[3] The Committee made a number of proposals about widening access to learning opportunities, concentrating on funding, financial support for students, the setting of targets, clarity of advice and guidance and the development of local partnerships. The report also discussed some fundamental issues concerning basic principles.

The Committee was clear in its belief that 'further education should continue to be firmly rooted in the local community'. Local providers of further education were encouraged to collaborate to identify and meet the needs of their community, and to work out strategies for involving individuals and groups whose lives are at present untouched by education.

'Education must be at the heart of any inspired project for regeneration in Britain,' Kennedy says. 'It should be a springboard for the revitalisation that our communities so urgently need... In a social landscape where there is a growing gulf between those who have and those who have not, the importance of social cohesion cannot be ignored.'

All learning is valuable, she says. 'In a system so caught up in what is measurable, we can forget that learning is also about problem-solving, learning to learn, acquiring the capability for intelligent choice in exercising personal responsibility. It is a weapon against poverty. It is the route to participation and active citizenship.'

Kennedy's committee challenged the validity of the distinction made between vocational, accredited and non-vocational 'pleasure' courses. Tutors and organisers have always known that the so-called 'pleasure' courses are particularly useful in widening participation in education. Students who have failed at school are likely to perceive exams as threatening - yet another opportunity for failure. A non-accredited art, dance or health-related course can provide a comfortable way back into learning to learn. Then the new student, with confidence regained, can move on to vocational learning if he or she wishes - especially if such opportunities are available within the same building.

We live in a fast-changing society. 'Even a glimpse of the future provides incontrovertible evidence that we must widen our horizons. The pace of technological innovation within the world of work continues to accelerate phenomenally quickly. Changes in information technology are akin to the introduction of the printing press and the industrial revolution, both of which precipitated revolutions in the speed of learning. More and more people need to achieve higher-level knowledge, understanding and skills. Everyone must acquire different knowledge, improved understanding and new skills throughout their working lives. Failure to take this agenda forward will worsen the already wide gap between those people and their families who know and can do, and those who do not know and cannot do,' reported the Committee. Further education, with its experience of designing new courses, working with part-time staff and in partnership was seen by the Committee to be in an advantageous position to respond to changing needs. 'However, there is also a growing disquiet that the new ethos has encouraged colleges not just to be businesslike but to perform as if they were businesses' Kennedy warned. It is certainly not a coincidence that after the report's publication, opportunities for effective partnership working increased and competition for students, although it did not disappear, reduced considerably.

'Conventional structures of work are changing at a rapid rate ... developments in new technology impact on domestic and community life as well as the workplace,' reported the Committee. Grey Friars staff had for a long time believed that in order to cope with the challenges of changing society adults need to have local educational provision which they can access at a variety of levels at times to suit their working and/or domestic lives. It is only if this is in place that there can be any possibility of meeting the aim of the National Advisory Council for Education and Training Targets that three in five of the adult workforce should be qualified to at least NVQ level 3 - quite apart from the possibility of remedying that 'one in six of the population over the age of 16 has serious problems with basic skills.' Basic Skills Agency.[4]

Kennedy's report makes it clear that, 'The hallmark of a college's success is, as it should be, public trust, satisfaction of the "stakeholders" and esteem rather than profitability. These colleges do not see students as "consumers", or learning merely as "training".'

Grey Friars has always worked according to the belief that an ethos of partnership and support must be in evidence if participation in education is to be widened. Adult education is not simply a matter of designing and presenting courses. People need a friendly face in reception, a friendly voice on the phone line. A poll taken by Grey Friars in the 1980s made it clear - the best form of advertising is recommendation, which in turn depends upon being treated well. As a result, the enrolment and information systems were changed and more reception and information staff were engaged.

The same principle is true in the classroom. Students need their tutors to take an interest in their progress and to stay in touch when gaps in attendance occur, supporting a successful return. What promotes regular attendance is both the quality of learning and the quality of relationships with tutor and fellow students. The buzz, the pleasure, the feeling that they've been doing something worthwhile, that they've achieved something – and that they *belong*.

In June 2004 the National Institute of Adult Continuing Education held a conference called 'Kennedy – Seven Years On'. Although much has changed since the report was published, adult educators are aware that much good practice arising from *Learning Works* is still relevant, but is at risk. Much valuable effort will be wasted if the decision-makers and the sector itself do not avoid, in the words of the Kennedy report, 'too limited a definition of learners, and too narrow a focus on the range of learning opportunities'.

Alan Tuckett, the director of the National Institute for Adult Continuing education (NIACE) spoke about the importance of inclusiveness of vision - everybody matters, not just those who fit easily into categories. We mustn't narrow the range of routes to learning, otherwise we will exclude people. He stressed the importance of adult education being appropriate to its own geographical area.

The curriculum doesn't begin and end with what happens in the classroom. It needs support around it. He emphasised that adults need adult systems, not systems designed for young people. He said that we need to value the culture of learning more in this country and that we must not spend all our educational money on the privileged. He wished to remind everybody of the importance of community outreach – taking learning to the learners.

Helena Kennedy addressed the conference. She said it was important to have periodic reviews to re-energise the debate. It was necessary to address educational aspects of regeneration and social cohesion, the division between rich and poor. Education is a powerful way to bridge gaps. She regretted that resources had not come through in the way that she had hoped. She spoke of the importance of repairing the faults of the past and making it possible for people to have a second chance. It was a responsibility that we all bore and shared, to give chances to other people to enable them to shape their own lives. In a comment from the floor someone pointed out that widening participation is contradictory to measurable outcomes. Kennedy agreed: 'That which is valuable can not always be measured. Forcing learning activities to fit ways of measuring can be a corruption of what we are in business for,' she stated.

Ivan Lewis, Minister for Skills and Vocational Education (now Minister for Young People and Skills) spoke of the unprecedented level of investment by the present government. Lifelong learning, now meaning from cradle to grave, was back at the heart of government strategy. The government aims for a fairer society and a more economically successful one, offering 'the dignity of self-improvement'. Getting parents and grandparents back into learning has an impact on children and grandchildren; we need family and community aspirations. People need literacy skills to function socially and economically in the community. Lewis wanted to give emphasis to vocational as well as academic skills, which would be paid for by the employer and learner, as well as the state. He was proud of the government's achievements - lives were being transformed. The job for life had gone, and the focus for education had to be employability for life.

Frances O'Grady, Deputy General Secretary of the TUC, said that seven million people in the UK are functionally illiterate. It was a human loss, with people unable to fulfil their potential. She mentioned the close correlation between how skilled you are and how healthy you are, using this as an argument for expanding education among those who've lost out. Unionised workers were more likely to get training. The TUC wanted to promote education, and hoped to have helped 500,000 workers back into education by the end of the decade. It had 22,000 'union learning reps', well placed to get workers who needed it back into education.

Colin Flint, the Associate Director for FE, NIACE, in summing up, said that we need a campaign for a learning society. Adult education is about all learners and their life chances.

And that is determinedly what Grey Friars is about. It continues to forge ahead in its brave attempt to provide the services that its community needs through its comprehensive curriculum, putting its ideals of social cohesion and justice into practice. Above all, it continues to provide a wide range of accessible learning experiences, so that learning can improve life for everybody.   [MF]

Government targets tend to be simplistic. In former Education Secretary Charles Clarke's 2004 Grant Letter to the LSC the present targets are set out, starting with 'All young people should reach age 19 ready for skilled employment or higher education'.

Within that wider aim are some measurable objectives. First, by 2008 60% of those aged 16 years are expected to achieve level 2 (equivalent of 5 GCSEs grades A* to C). It is intended that the proportion of those aged 19 who achieve at least level 2 should increase by 5% by 2008. The proportion of young people not in education, training or work should decrease by 2% by 2010.

The Government also aims to 'tackle the adult skills gap'. This will be done by 'increasing the number of adults with the skills required for employability and progression to higher levels of training through two main targets: improving the basic skills levels of 2.25 million adults by 2010 (milestone for 2007 is 1.5 million); and reducing by 40% by 2010 the number of adults in the workforce who lack level 2 qualifications'.

Unlike previous Remit and Grant Letters, Clarke's latest letter makes no specific mention of the wider curriculum for adults. His own Remit Letter of 2003-4 stated, 'It is important for the Council to develop a long term vision for the future planning and funding of adult and community learning (and) secure the availability of a coherent, accessible, high quality range of opportunities for study which does not lead to qualifications'.

Education Secretary Estelle Morris in the 2002-3 letter told the LSC to 'Increase demand for learning by adults ... Contribute to delivering the Government's Strategy for Neighbourhood Renewal by supplying a revitalised adult and community learning sector'.

David Blunkett's original Remit Letter to the LSC in 2000 stated 'I look to the Council to increase the demand for learning by adults and to increase the supply of flexible, high-quality opportunities to meet their needs. This is central to our goal of a learning society - a society in which everyone can share in the benefits of learning, enabling people to discover new talents, stretching their creativity and widening their opportunities .... This includes provision for the growing proportion of older people'.

It is debatable whether researchers will find a way of assessing wider effects of learning that are acceptable to the Treasury as well as the policy-makers. If the results of research made it possible to convey the true value of adult learning in ways to which funding bodies could relate - or at least in ways less easy to dismiss as marginal – it would certainly challenge the present balance of distribution.

The negative effect of marginalisation

Those who have experienced the positive results of adult education (many of which come from non-quantifiable elements such as non-exam arts and cultural activities) along with those who have fought hard to have it recognised for its value to society, are amazed and angered when it is dismissed as marginal and therefore disposable. The spectre of 'conventional wisdom' with all its myths and platitudes still comes to the fore from time to time.

Beleaguered ministers and officials are likely to make defensive statements such as 'when it comes to a choice between helping people to train for a job and funding someone to paint pictures, I know where my money would go!' We can also expect the occasional blasting in the press when an ill-informed reporter makes fun of a subject, quite likely to be an 'outreach' project ("Makeup lessons on the rates"), or a more politically-motivated comment ("Public subsidy for Spanish villa owners' language classes"). But it is more worrying when negative messages come from within the educational establishment.

The 1990s gave a whole new language to the world of adult education. After the abortive attempt of Secretary of State for Education Kenneth Clarke to remove government funding and make all non-accredited adult learning financially self-supporting, a place had to be found for it in the new post-school education system.

Treating 'traditional' adult education as the add-on it had become, the new Further Education Funding Council (FEFC) invented terminology to describe it. Terms such as 'out-of-sector activity' joined 'non-vocational' and 'non-accredited' as descriptors for types of courses. Later, the more precise term, 'non-schedule 2', categorised individual courses where the subject may be academic, but the course did not lead to an outcome described in Schedule 2 to the Further and Higher Education Act 1992.

'Non-incorporated' and 'non-sector' were used to describe the organisations which specialised in 'non-schedule 2' courses and the term 'college' was reserved for incorporated institutions. Thus Grey Friars, despite being a college with governance, a management system with departments, its own premises, a delegated budget – and a substantial amount of work which came within Schedule 2 to the Act, was referred to as an 'external institution' and was not afforded the status of 'college'. Indeed, in order to receive funds from the FEFC for its Schedule 2 work (such as GCSEs, A-Levels, City & Guilds, RSA and other exam subjects, plus the nationally- prioritised literacy and numeracy work) Grey Friars had to be 'sponsored' and its bid for funds ratified by an FE Corporation. In this case sponsorship was negotiated with the Colchester Institute and the Sixth Form College – both being 'proper' colleges. This demotion of Grey Friars was received with incredulity by senior staff and governors – especially in the light of the high academic standards achieved over recent years.

Grey Friars' national standing for academic awards was (until the reorganisation of examination bodies) literally second to none. For example, the achievements of 1993 were applauded in a press release from the Associated Examining Board which declared Grey Friars 'Top of the league for top-performing A-Level students ... for the fourth time since the awards began in 1986 the college has claimed one of the medals ... Backwell School in Bristol follows closely behind with three ... Oundle School, Peterborough and Chippenham College have two medals each.'

The list of top academic achievers who studied at Grey Friars is impressive. In 1988, Anna Debska was declared the 'Top languages Candidate' in the A Level group of language subjects for her French result. In 1991 Ann McPhail was the Business Studies 'Top A Level Achiever'. 1992 saw Zoe Thomas take the English A Level 'Best Performance' prize.

In 1993, Katherine Wells gained the Business Studies A Level highest mark in the country. In the same year another four students were honoured: one in the top five of 14,733 candidates in Business Studies A Level and two other students in the top five of 1,133 candidates in Economic & Social History A Level. Grey Friars also had a student in the top five out of 15,260 candidates in Psychology.

In 2000, Steven Parkin's results put him in the top five Economic and Social History A Level students in the country. In 2001, Marian Pooran was awarded a 'Highly Commended' certificate for her work in Fashion Design in the City & Guilds awards.

2002 saw Bridget Rippingdale and Lindsay Harrison both gain a place in the top ten students out of 2,700 candidates in GCSE Psychology.

Rapid Growth

In spite of the new hierarchical system damaging its budget (the two-tier categorisation led to two-tier funding and of course Grey Friars received the lower tariffs – even for the same outcomes!) and its place in the educational system (it soon became apparent that anything perceived as 'traditional' adult education was relegated to the lower division) Grey Friars managed to develop rapidly over a ten-year period. Staff re-established Grey Friars' reputation as a significant provider of high-quality adult learning of all kinds - and in the process increased its direct interaction with local communities through many innovative activities.

As well as incorporating the Wilson Marriage Centre (in danger of becoming redundant after its original youth, community and youth-training fell outside funding priorities) Grey Friars was reaching into local areas. Staff, for example, rented accommodation in the heart of the St Anne's, Greenstead, Highwoods, Old Heath and Monkwick. Staff also used a travelling classroom, built on a lorry chassis as a go-anywhere teaching facility. Funding received was low given the breadth and quality of activity undertaken, but by planning strategically (including, of course, a process of prioritising spending) staff managed to balance the needs of funding bodies with the requirements of local communities and maintained a comprehensive curriculum.

Throughout the period of the FEFC's control of government funding, senior staff resolved to make it 'impossible to see the join' between the 'officially-funded' part of the curriculum and the more traditional adult education programme. Indeed, many Grey Friars managers felt that these parts of the curriculum were totally interchangeable, with students 'progressing' in all directions – widening their experiences as if exploring a web and not just climbing the academic ladder.

In the present era, with the Learning and Skills Council (LSC) now setting national and local priorities as well as distributing funding, Grey Friars still aims to maintain its comprehensive curriculum in the belief that any division of an adult curriculum is at its best artificial and cumbersome and at worst over-bureaucratic, divisive and wasteful.

[MF/AS]

References

1   Occasional Research Papers (2001-2005) Various authors School of Continuing Education, Birkbeck College, University of London www.bbk.ac.uk/ce/research

2   Russell, Sir Lionel (1973) *Adult Education: A Plan for Development* HMSO London

3   Kennedy, Helena (1997) *Learning Works – Widening Participation in Further Education* FEFC Coventry

4   Basic Skills Agency (2004) *Corporate Brochure* BSA New Oxford Street London www.basic-skills.co.uk

10

Social and Professional Links

In addition to taught courses, Grey Friars has developed the kind of additional activity which is highly valued by local people. College staff, however, struggle to convey, quantify and assess the value of its contribution in terms acceptable to the LSC and, increasingly and most depressingly, to Local Education Authorities.

The Grey Friars Guild

Some of Grey Friars' most endearing characteristics are founded on the belief that learning should really be lifelong. This belief is translated into action in both curriculum and extra-mural activities.

One of these additional activities has just celebrated its twentieth anniversary. The Grey Friars Guild exists for people who are retired and not in full time work. To belong to the Guild members need to have followed at least two terms of a course in the college. The Guild's aim is to provide fellowship through running a variety of social and educational events. On a weekly basis throughout the term a meeting is called in the Grey Friars hall with an uncomplicated agenda; coffee, announcements and for an hour or so a speaker or an activity. It concludes with questions and a vote of thanks and then members can stay for lunch in the refectory and afternoon classes that have been negotiated with the college.

The Guild is self-financing. Members pay a yearly subscription of £8 and run fundraising activities like bring and buy, raffles and selling tea and coffee during meetings.

The autumn term of 2004 started with the 20th Birthday party and ended on December 10th with a Christmas party. In between those events, members learned about steamboats, local youth work, the Leonard Cheshire Homes, Guy Fawkes, and aloe vera, nature's healer – following a tradition engaging a diverse range of speakers every year.

For the 20th birthday party the hall was full - at least 70 of the active members must have been there. Principal Alan Skinner gave a speech. He has been involved since the beginning in 1984 when Anne McEwen, a staff member active in the Members' Association, researched similar activities and set up the Guild, following an initiative by the Area Community Education officer of the time, John Thompson. On such occasions, Alan likes pithy, short speeches about the educational and social significance of the class, group or organisation and when he'd finished we all toasted the Guild in sparkling wine. An accompanying spread on the trestle tables was one of those occasions when each contributing member outdoes the next with tasty nibbles. A buzz of cheerful conversation filled the hall.

On the display boards on the dais were documents illustrating two decades of Guild history. They were drawn from the careful collection of photographs, newspaper cuttings and programmes collected by Jill Butcher. She had taught dressmaking at Grey Friars for 25 years and joined the Guild after leaving. Now she is the treasurer. I was sorry not to have seen the only performance, in December 1986, of 'Ah, Cruel Fate,' a mini-drama by Richard Tideman. And there have been plenty of similar creative events since then. In 2004 there were 75 active members. The Guild cannot expand because of the capacity of the hall.

Bernard Poole, who had to take an early retirement from local government, settled in Colchester because he had worked in the district although he and his wife Beryl came originally from Manchester. Early retirement gave him time for his hobbies of piano playing and gardening and he found joining the Guild in 1984 provided him with plenty of activity. He is grateful for this because he had not particularly wished for retirement. His name features in many of the early productions. He reflects rather sadly that there was more enthusiasm in the early days. There are fewer male members nowadays, he says and some ladies can be a bit shy. Bernard takes the view that the changes in the Guild are only reflecting changes in society in general.

One of the members, a widow, told me how much the weekly meetings meant to her. The Guild, its motto being Fellowship and Friendship, helps her to cope with solitude now that her children have left home and her partner has died. She takes an afternoon Yoga class. Grey Friars runs special Keep Fit classes for the active elderly. And many Guild members follow painting courses. Watercolours are particularly favoured.

In 1995 when the Guild celebrated VE day 50 years on, apart from members wearing authentic 1945 clothes, they also had a collection of memorabilia that any social historian would envy - ration books, clothing coupons, gas masks and genuine NAAFI style refreshments served on a table decorated with mini Union Jacks . The memorabilia included many objects some of the members knew from personal experience.

The photographs of members' activities show the increasingly rare arts and crafts that require time, effort and enthusiasm to be kept alive against a flood of cheap plastics and ready-made everything: decoupage, eggshell decorating, millinery, cake icing. Crafts that can disappear without efforts to keep them alive. Not one of the obvious aims of the Grey Friars Guild, but certainly one of its outcomes. The crafts in which Guild members participate usually belong to a less rushed era. It takes many hours to decorate and varnish a duck egg in the Fabergé manner.

For the year's penultimate meeting of the Guild, the choral class came for a Christmas concert. The choir is taught and led by college tutor Sheila Scott. Attending school at Grey Friars in the 1940s she recalls assembly in the same hall where she is now leading the choir. The concert lasts one hour. Then the audience join in more popular carols. The atmosphere is warm, friendly and a little nostalgic. Everyone in the Guild is over 55, many considerably older, and most members of the choir are also older women. 'We always need new blood,' Sheila tells me, and points out two recent younger recruits.

[DS]

Co-operation and collaboration

Principal Alan Skinner sees communication and involvement as an essential element of any service which has 'community' in the title – especially one that also purports to be community-driven. In addition to the normal extra-curricular activities of exhibitions, journeys, foreign exchanges, clubs and societies, and the provision of reference library and study facilities, Grey Friars encourages more formal participation.

The Members' Association is an important forum for people wishing to become involved in the life of the college, students, staff and affiliated members. It has always had its own identity, its own finances and run its own affairs. That it is separate from, yet highly influential in the affairs of, the college is an important element in its success.

The standard activity of fund-raising through a series of commercial or social events has been supplemented from time to time by intense political activity where public opinion can be expressed in relation to adult education.

The Association has been directly involved in college life over the decades. It was highly influential in assuring the continuation of the crèche in the 1980s by giving substantial financial support. Further financial aid was given to a range of courses and subjects in the provision of resources and materials such as art and crafts equipment and specialist swimming equipment. But the most significant single success for the Association must surely be the campaign to save Grey Friars as the local flagship of adult education. In the mid-1980s, Essex County Council officials were planning to move all the youth social events, youth training scheme and adult education into one building, the Wilson Marriage Centre, and to sell off the Grey Friars site.

Intense lobbying, public meetings, a press campaign and a number of meetings with people from all spheres of interest eventually drew a statement from Essex County Council announcing that Grey Friars would remain as the area's adult college. The youth centre in Brook Street was sold for housing, as was the former East Ward school, home of ECC's youth training scheme and those services moved into Wilson Marriage school. Grey Friars was saved, with much credit due to leading lights in the Association, such as Peter Bailey, Anne McEwen, Bob Walker and Jill Butcher.

The next significant mobilisation came in the early 1990s at the time of the Further and Higher Education Bill. A main element in the Bill was the proposal that all adult education which did not have a vocational or examination purpose (ie the whole of the traditional, liberal adult education curriculum) should be self-funding, that is paid for (resources, teachers, administration) entirely by the students. To this end, the Bill set out to split the curriculum into two distinct sections. Although nation-wide protest and lobbying forced the Secretary of State for Education,

Kenneth Clarke, to make a u-turn on the self-funding issue and to continue to allow public subsidy for traditional adult education subjects, when the Bill became law, the curriculum remained split in two. That legacy remains to the present day.

'What is not widely known,' Alan Skinner told us, 'is that the government bucked the normal trend and started off the Bill in the House of Lords. This meant that adult educators had to mobilise themselves very quickly and we formed a group of principals from all over the country. We each took responsibility for contacting a number of Lords. I remember a very congenial morning spent with the late Lord Alport, who was very supportive of our cause, despite the Bill being originated by his own party. We worked on an amendment which would give colleges like Grey Friars direct access to funding without having to be sponsored. The amendment was lost by one vote – how different things might have been!'

The Members' Association sets off to join the Westminster Rally against the 1992 Education Act.

A national and international perspective is given to the work of the Association by its membership of the Educational Centres Association (ECA). This body, of over 80 years standing, has its roots in the 'educational settlements' of the universities which were set up to take adult education out into the heart of communities. Its distinguishing feature is the equal standing of organisers, students, tutors and others involved in supporting adult learning.

This fits very comfortably with the Grey Friars ethos. The national committee includes students and tutors at the highest levels. The only hierarchy is that of the Association's own organisation as a registered charity and the need for people to take a range of responsibilities – not of background, sector, profession or educational attainment. Notable Grey Friars members nationally and regionally have been Ann McEwen who was a tireless worker for the Members' Association and the ECA during the 1980s, Sue Tye, an occupational therapist and long standing volunteer, who is a current member of the regional committee and principal Alan Skinner, the current ECA national vice-chairman.

Howard Leyshon, Margaret Bearman, Diana McLeod and Colin Kirby-Green have been some of the many Grey Friars people who have given well-received presentations at national conferences. The College has also hosted a regional conference with presentations by student Marion Walls and Winston Browne, who was responsible for kick-starting educational activities in the heart of his local housing estate.

Learning in the Heart of the Community

Winston was the driving force in a co-operative arrangement which grew from residents of the Greenstead estate wishing to take part in a range of positive, sustainable activities on their own patch. A group of supporters and advisers was set up to include local people, people from the Benefits Agency, Libraries, voluntary services and Grey Friars. The group was chaired by a local councillor and linked with the Borough Council's regeneration activities. A series of events, classes and drop-in sessions was held at a range of venues.

This was then moved forward when the College leased a flat on the estate. This in itself required a collaborative effort to research a suitable location and to overcome bureaucratic issues such as planning permission and legal requirements. Participation increased immediately despite the location being in an area notorious for its uneasy atmosphere. 'This was a deliberate choice, albeit rather a gamble,' Alan Skinner said afterwards. 'The intention was to show that positive, productive activities could take place in any part of the estate. We intended to have a year of community-based learning activities and then hand over to the new Community Association Centre, being built with regeneration funds.' Eventually, Grey Friars staff and local people were able to take part in a range of awareness-raising projects lasting two years. 'For me, this was one of the highlights of the 1990s,' he said. 'It took me out of the office, away from the computer and reminded me of the practical aspects of community learning. It was a pleasure to be introduced to people who readily invited me into their homes, spoke to me about their ambitions and showed how keen they were to be participants – not passive recipients. The whole experience reminded me of the true roots of community education.'

The estate now has a substantial community building with a range of activities supported by voluntary and statutory agencies. The adjacent library hosts a branch of Colchester's Signpost – a charity supporting people seeking work. These all have an education and training element. In common with the neighbouring St Anne's estate (referred to in chapter 3) local people are keen to participate in and prove sustainable, projects which hitherto have been considered short-term.

CALCAG

Colchester Adult Learning Continuing Access Group is the College's registered charity working to support the widest possible access to adult learning opportunities throughout the community. It aims to remove barriers to learning for people with access difficulties and disabilities and older people especially.

It began as the Grey Friars Lift Fund and became a fully-fledged charitable body when it was seen that the 'corporatisation' of the County Council would render it impossible for any group within one of its colleges to have its own identity or to retain control of monies it raised. Creating an identity separate from the Council, then using that identity to forge a 'partnership of equals' with Council officials seemed to be the answer. In this way, CALCAG could interact with the Council on its own terms, choose where it directed its money and, importantly, ask the kind of questions that employees feel unable to.

Janet Fulford, a former mayor of Colchester chairs the group. John Knight of the Grey Friars Guild and staff members Jenny Jones and Jon Williams give valuable organisational support. Colchester MP, Bob Russell, is president. However, in keeping with the tradition of Grey Friars, the few may provide the inspiration and guidance, but it is the collective support that is crucial. Contributions have come from hundreds of people. Donations, each worth many hundreds of pounds, have come from groups such as the local Open Gardens scheme, the Grey Friars choir, the Guild, the Members' Association, the WEA, Concorde Singers, various course groups, sponsored walks and raffles. A range of personal donations have come from bequests, donations in memory and impromptu gifts both large and small – all greatly appreciated and handled with the greatest of respect by the Trustees.

The Colchester Learning Shop

The idea of a Learning Shop arose from the need to combat the competitive environment engendered by the Further Education Funding Council (FEFC) in the late 1990s.

Several FE institutions in Colchester sought to cater for the needs of post-16 education. Painfully aware of their precarious financial state (and their inability to access grants and contracts due to lacking 'proper college' status) the senior managers at Grey Friars recognised that it made far more sense for all these institutions to work together, pooling and targeting their resources instead of wasting them by competing against each other.

This was not as inevitable as it may seem for, paradoxically, this under-funded adult college did very well for enrolments during the competitive years. 'We have always been able to tune in to the needs of local people and have developed not only an expertise in researching and planning, but can also tap into a vast network of community and voluntary support in passing the word. We have spent hardly anything on traditional forms of advertising new ventures,' remarked current principal Alan Skinner.

In order to achieve some coherence in what Alan calls 'the area curriculum' and engender a more co-operative approach, Grey Friars tried to persuade the Borough Council to declare Colchester a "Learning Borough". This was supported by senior staff from the Colchester Institute (the local college of further and higher education). Their involvement was crucial, as they were in a position to access funding, being 'inside' the corporate FE sector. They resourced meetings to explore the ideas and delegated staff to facilitate research.

'The ultimate goal would be the development of a network, essentially a partnership, which would oversee an "area curriculum" - the whole range of courses, educational activities, training schemes and assessment opportunities planned and presented as a coherent offer. In this way no provider need lose its identity, but was to be willing to stand up to peer scrutiny should their programmes be non-strategic, cherry-picking or deliberately commercially competitive,' Alan explained.

This was certainly a new approach. The previous regime set up by a government which promoted 'the market' as a way of sorting out choice and quality in public services was still very much in evidence. The conversion, at a later date, from the FEFC (purely a funding body) to the LSC (intended to be a planning *and* funding body) should have made the situation even better. The LSC was charged with responsibility for sorting out needs and the balance of provision. But it transpired that there was still an urgent need for local co-operation because in the event the enormity of the task seemed problematical for the LSC. For example (possibly due to the difficulty of meeting targets) they allowed a private provider from another county to set up IT centres in Colchester, without the knowledge of the local partnership.

Frustrated by slow progress, colleagues decided to push ahead independently. Their aim was to develop a partnership which would exemplify the European 'Learning City' ethos, where 'joined-up thinking' would ensure that public agencies and the business world would address the varied learning needs at all stages of life and engender a 'learning society' committed to a culture of continuous exploration of learning. This would hopefully energise other organizations in the area to see learning and training as natural activities, rather than impositions to be endured.

A perfect opportunity came when the Further Education Funding Council (FEFC) converted its "competitiveness fund" (to which incorporated FE colleges could apply for support in marketing their courses) to a "collaboration fund" (which would only be accessed by partnerships). It didn't matter that it was only open to application from those 'inside the sector' - the Institute was willing to host the project and worked with Grey Friars and others 'outside the sector' to secure funding for research, feasibility studies and start-up activities. Staff from Colchester Institute's Professional Training Centre were significant drivers of this project with Judy Sexton and Clare Birch tireless in their efforts to make the dream a reality.

The Learning Shop was eventually set up as a company and a charity. The founding chairman of the Board was Alan Skinner, the Grey Friars principal, the company secretary was Peter Johnston from the University of Essex, the finance director was Ann Seaman from Anglia Polytechnic University, plus other senior members from Colchester Institute, the Open University, the Sixth Form College and, crucially, as this was to be a community-wide project, the Borough Council.

A large town-centre shop was identified. A lease and planning permission for change of use was eventually gained. Alan Skinner had to present the case before the Planning Committee because the application had initially been rejected by Borough Council Planning Officers. All partners contributed cash and services, but the Shop was to operate independently. Over the four years that it has been established, it has achieved a reputation as an 'honest broker' for information, advice and guidance (IAG) at all levels of local people's educational and training aspirations.

The first manager, Rachel Brown, facilitated inter-agency liaison in various outreach activities including, for example, organising advisers to accompany the Grey Friars travelling classroom to supermarkets and industrial estates, as well as attending fairs, country shows and neighbourhood fetes.

A vast range of information and advice (including individual guidance appointments) is freely available to the public, and the Shop's premises now host an IT learning centre. The Shop has developed into a fount of knowledge on local education and training needs, all recorded and analysed and available in reports to board meetings.

An additional, confidential, service feeds back to individual partner institutions the unsolicited comments made about them by the public. These prove to be an invaluable source of information on a partner's public profile, and have contributed to staff training and quality assurance processes.

The potential is there for development of an area curriculum strategy through feedback of detailed data analysis, leading to collaborative planning and pilot projects. There have already been some major moves on rationalising provision of GCSE and 'A' Level courses, as well as the development of new approaches to IT and 'outreach' community-based activities, most notably as collaborations between Grey Friars and the Institute. The partnership must however guard against complacency: not only do projects need to be re-visited in a strategic fashion, but the implications of an 'area curriculum' concept need identifying carefully.

Initial frustrations caused by barriers to *real* partnerships (that is, partnerships of equals making a real difference to the educational offering) have been only partially addressed, however, and this gives a real sense of concern that opportunities may be wasted. Initial euphoria at getting together the first-ever collaborative partnership between the major post-16 providers plus the Local Authority (Colchester Borough Council – which is not a Local Education Authority – that is Essex County Council's role) has been tempered by unanswered (so far) questions such as:

When will the local Learning and Skills Council (LLSC) be able to engage more fully in supporting the Shop and are there other funding bodies who may contribute? There is no direct LSC or LEA funding for the service despite its potential to help in the LLSC planning role.

How long will the partners be able to sustain large contributions from their already-stretched budgets, bearing in mind that the Shop is of necessity not a direct marketing tool for partners' programmes?

Will the funding system specifically for Information Advice and Guidance activities be reliable enough to enable staff to plan ahead in the knowledge of what will be government-funded and what will have to be funded from other sources?

Will the new proposals for the funding of non-accredited adult learning (long overdue at the time of writing) severely reduce the number of entry points for people taking up learning after a long gap?

Will the sector be allowed to settle into a period of stability so that valuable services not necessarily contributing directly and immediately to government targets, such as crèches and support services for non-exam students, be sustained?

Will there be sufficient stability to enable providers to sustain (or confidently enter into) meaningful partnerships?

All at Grey Friars are very keen to continue to support the Learning Shop both as a customer-orientated service to the local community and as a means of bringing together relevant parties in order to collaborate in a meaningful and practical partnership. It is the key to helping local people make sense of a complicated education and training system.

It is a co-operative, coherent and accessible organisation and managers and governors at Grey Friars do not want to see such potential being wasted. It would be very sad if it were to be sacrificed on the altar of inter-sectoral politics, competition or bureaucracy.

11

Governors

The College Governors in 2000.

I'm in a lofty Edwardian classroom in the Wilson Marriage Centre which was once a school but is now used for adult education. I'm here to see how the governors, who are responsible for overseeing the work of the College, conduct their meeting. Alan Skinner says I can stay throughout except when staff personal issues are discussed.

The atmosphere before the meeting is jovial. Refreshments are spartan, three jugs of squash and no biscuits. There are six women and seven men which is not representative of the gender balance in the college. However, it's good compared with many other governing bodies in further education.

An officer from County Hall has come to the meeting. He's from Adult Community Learning, Essex, part of the Libraries, Culture and Adult Learning Service Group. The County Council is reviewing all of its property holdings with land disposals very much in the frame. Without a word to the principal or governors, officials have already been to look at the Grey Friars perimeter wall and the land it encloses. The entire area is a conservation zone and it is thought unlikely that the land could be used for building. Attention is now on the whole site, including the college buildings. The official tells us that there are certain buildings that the council 'may want to keep, even if they are old.'

Janet Fulford the vice chairman says that there would be a public outcry if Grey Friars were to be sold. Of the women governors present Janet was the one who played the most significant part in the discussions.

There is a general agreement that it would reflect very badly on the County Council if they did try to axe Grey Friars. It is further agreed that Grey Friars would fit well into the Borough Council's proposed new St Botolph's development. Alan Skinner recalls an impractical proposal made fifteen years earlier that Grey Friars, the Youth Service and Youth Training Scheme should all squeeze into the Wilson Marriage building.

The meeting progresses in a polite and orderly fashion, but I begin to sense a tension between the priorities of County Hall and those of Grey Friars. No one says so openly, but it seems to me that County Hall is seeking to exert greater administrative control and Grey Friars is resisting the pressure; trying to retain some independence in order to better serve the local community.

Alan Skinner's report is clear and succinct. He wants to look beyond the present with a fully-costed business plan for the college, based on a strategic plan for the adult education service. In financial terms it is necessary to plan for more than one year ahead otherwise there is no guarantee that curriculum plans can be resourced. Grey Friars has been existing on an annual 'net-nil' budget (that is, managing only to achieve a balance of income against expenditure - with no surplus available to carry forward) for some years with the obvious dangers which that entails.

The governors listen attentively. Alan goes on. 'There is a real need for a proper business plan. Let's do this straight after inspection and not keep waiting for funding announcements. As soon as we can, we must convert the plethora of 'plans' into a clear and realistically-costed business strategy. Funding delegated to the colleges should reflect the actual work undertaken and there should be capacity for integrated curriculum development across the non-accredited/accredited divide. If we are forced to produce a narrow curriculum we risk losing important routes of entry for reluctant and disaffected learners.'

The officer reminds governors of the effect of 'performance indicators and targets' and explains the LEA's requirement to write a 3-year plan and an annual 'Adult Learning Plan' for the Learning and Skills Council as well as a plan for the County Council to enable it to judge how the adult education service is meeting County Council priorities. Governors list all the various documents which colleges must produce including self-assessment reports. These latter reports are then amalgamated to produce one Service-wide report. Curriculum and other plans received the same treatment. The officer agrees that the production of these documents is repetitious and onerous.

The most important business of the meeting appears in the Budget Report. The college is seriously under-funded for the range of activity it has developed. Funding has been generated to a large degree by the number of 'learning hours' provided, but the college is not to receive resources commensurate with its output. 'Top slicing' is required of all college incomes to pay for the costs of managing the overall LEA service centrally. Alan Skinner comments that Grey Friars doesn't even get its proportional amount of the already top-sliced income, due to the method of distribution. It doesn't help that the funding is split according to curriculum category. Whereas originally colleges knew where they stood in relation to their own programmes, now the LSC deals only with County Hall to which all funds are sent prior to redistribution.

The officer explains a further complication. Grey Friars has constantly 'over-achieved' its targets in the further education (more highly funded) categories. Some governors look incredulous and ask how it can be a bad thing, 'punishable' by withheld funding, to educate more people than was originally required.

The answer is that the LSC contracted only for a certain amount of work and more people came forward than the funds allowed for. Alan Skinner explains that in past years the college budget was flexible and money could be transferred from one part of the curriculum to support another. Now, however, the costs of meeting management, administrative, inspection and monitoring requirements, plus the need to resource improvements in accommodation and equipment have drained any small surpluses gained from project funding and entrepreneurial activities, such as running the car park and catering as businesses. And it gets worse.

There is more bad news. Last year there were fewer non-accredited student hours generated in comparison to previous performances, so that category of funding has been decreased.

What governors find difficult to accept, however, is that Grey Friars still provides a greater amount of activity than any other college and has in the past contributed funds to boost other colleges. A 'safeguarding scheme' had operated under the LEA's previous 'formula budget' arrangements and Grey Friars had been 'top sliced' to contribute to a redistribution of funds for some years. Is this not time for some payback? Apparently not. There is a real fear around the room that decreasing funding could result in ever-decreasing student numbers, which could put Grey Friars into a spiral of decline.

On the budget plans there is an item about Grey Friars needing a new IT centre. Also, there are only *estimated* sums against some categories for staff costs. Alan Skinner says that he cannot predict how much staff time will be used up in 'outside' bureaucratic requirements such as county-wide inspections, curriculum meetings, training, monitoring exercises, quality assurance initiatives, management meetings and myriad other non-Colchester specific matters. Grey Friars is living on a financial knife edge. In response, governors suggest an immediate review of charges for services as well as an increase in fees for public parking on the Grey Friars site.

The meeting breaks up with promises to keep lines of communication open. A governor remarks to me that the actual teaching and the life and work of students hasn't featured much in the meeting. By this time we find ourselves in the corridor where we join in the relaxed, fulfilled and energised throng of students making their way out of the building after their evening class.   [DS]

Working together to overcome County-College tension

Alan Skinner talks about a plan he drew up to resolve some of the problems.

'It doesn't make sense to have governors if they aren't allowed to make descisions about the future of their college. I wanted to look at ways in which we could address the County Council's need to feel in control of a service for which it is responsible, whilst allowing the local people, the customers if you like, and the professionals it appoints to run the service to make it relevant to local communities. A compromise is required. There's no point asking for the involvement of people with high-quality educational experience and community commitment if you then don't give them the opportunity to use their skills and knowledge.

County could set up a system so that committed professionals and local people are able to work together creatively within a clear framework. Or it could set a clear agenda and appoint administrators to carry out its requirements to the letter. At present it has neither of these things. We cannot afford to have so many systems which repeat functions such as curriculum planning and quality assurance. Remember that the people carrying out these systems all have to be paid for out of the LSC's payments for educational activity. We need to get more money nearer to the learning in order to get a better return for our expenditure. This means fewer systems and fewer managers to run them. I'd like to see less county-wide administration and more resources reaching the colleges.

Some time ago I proposed a sort of contract between the County and the college principal and governors. It was a 'service-level agreement'.

It would work like this: The County Council would have an agreement with the college which sets out clearly the responsibilities of each party. At the same time, it would have overall responsibility and would set the strategy for the adult education service across the county. It would then devolve to the colleges the responsibility for implementing that strategy taking due regard of local needs and priorities. The governors and principal would be charged with meeting the County's strategic requirements, but would have a certain degree of freedom or flexibility so they could respond to the local situation. The overall contract would form a service-level agreement, within which every party would be sure of its remit. I see this as the only way to engender a productive partnership out of what could otherwise become a power struggle.

The system would have other advantages. All parties would have a clear remit, there would be less duplication of decision-making and administration and the result would be that more resources would be directed to where they should be, to where the teaching and learning takes place. Staff time could be directed towards ensuring efficient and smooth function at the interface between the Service and local people, rather than at the multiple interfaces that currently exist between County Hall and the colleges.

Instead of meeting to review plans, examine and explain differences in programme, performance and systems across the county, staff from the colleges could meet to share expertise and experience to improve learning for everybody. The Agreements would of course be monitored and performance adjudicated by a small group of people expert in the necessary type of analysis, leaving the educators to educate, the administrators to administrate – and the learners to learn.

I will continue to raise this idea as a way forward at the county meetings and hope that it will be seen as a means of addressing the needs of all parties. It makes economic sense. Today, there is more money devoted to post-16 education than ever before and yet far too much of it is being used, nationally and locally, to pay for systems of control rather than real educational activities.'

The Chairman of the Governors – Dr Ted Crunden

Having returned to Colchester after a rich and varied career in education and international organizations, Ted became actively involved in local politics as a Colchester Borough councillor and Essex County councillor. He became a governor and then chairman of Grey Friars' governing body, succeeding Ken Jones. Both men brought considerable experience to the governors. They had both held senior posts in education in a wide range of settings and were local politicians of significance, holding influential positions. Equally important was their commitment to the development of adult education opportunities relevant to local communities. Ted reflects below on the adult education service and what the future might hold.

'I am encouraged by the broad thrust of government policy and the words of Ivan Lewis, Minister for Skills and Vocational Education, who said that lifelong learning has the capacity to empower and liberate individual citizens, build the capacity of every community, and strengthen the economic and social foundations of our society.

However, what concerns me is that this vision is in danger of being

left to right: Dr Ted Crunden, Margaret Bearman (student governor), Peter Marsh (Members' Association chairman).

compromised by the bodies entrusted with its implementation who, I fear, may interpret it in too narrow a fashion.

Until recently, Essex County Council has had direct responsibility for funding and organising adult education. This has worked very successfully in Colchester through its Adult Community College, Grey Friars. Over the years the County Council has built up, with cross party support, an excellent reputation for its adult learning service throughout the county, which has been recognised as one of the best in the country.

However, in the country as a whole adult education provision varies in quality. In an effort to ensure that adult learning meets both local and national needs, the government has given the recently created Learning and Skills Council the remit for funding adult and community learning. In Essex this means that the Local Education Authorities (LEAs), Essex County Council and the unitary authorities of Southend and Thurrock, will still organise adult learning, but the funds they receive now come from LSC Essex, one of 49 local LSCs throughout the country.

The Government's Skills Strategy, published in 2003, sets out a plan to transform our national investment in skills and the LSC has recently published a consultation document (Fees, Funding and Learner Support) explaining how to apply the priorities and principles in the Skills Strategy to current provision - particularly for adult and community learning. However, education amounts to more than "skills", and while the Skills Strategy recognises and makes provision for "learning for personal development", there is a perception that the only adult learning which counts is that which contributes towards basic skills targets. NIACE (the National Institute for Adult Continuing Education) has pointed out that the LSC (including local LSCs) needs to adopt approaches that are more inclusive in order to address social as well as economic aspirations.

Adults undertake learning for personal development, for cultural aims and to enable them to participate in community development. Much of this learning is not intended to lead to the development of skills for work, although it may do so. The learning we do in private, in the community and outside work does extend into the workplace, and vice versa. Learning doesn't easily fit into little boxes. The skills that really matter are the transferable ones.

Those of us working with adults at grass roots level worry that the preoccupation with economic development and the emphasis on what can be measured, (e.g. participation rates and accreditation) could lead to a neglect of the needs of older learners. Ivan Lewis, the Minister for Skills, is a genuine enthusiast for the benefits of lifelong learning for everyone, but even he has said, in a meeting about lifelong learning, that "to insist that pensioners doing aerobics should be subject to an assessment is bonkers, but ensuring that they receive high quality instruction should be non-negotiable." Given demographic changes and an increasing number of older people, we should be recognising and valuing their experience and contribution.

Research carried out by the Centre for Research on the Wider Benefits of Learning shows how learning benefits health. Lifelong learning will surely play a crucial role in public health policy as people live longer into their 70s, 80s and 90s. Reducing the demands on social and health care budgets is important but should not be the only reason for the government to give its support to lifelong learning.

I said before that I'm concerned that there is a danger that the LSC's interpretation of what Ministers want will be too narrow. My concern is that the infrastructure for lifelong learners that has been developed since 1997 may be dismantled. NIACE believes that if Parliament wants to realise the full benefits of a culture of continuing education, it should challenge the LSC to adopt approaches that are more inclusive, more imaginative and more sophisticated in addressing social as well as economic aspirations for the country.

NIACE is increasingly concerned about the perception, sometimes encouraged by the LSC, that the only adult learning which counts is that which can be counted - predominantly towards basic skills targets or a "Level 2 entitlement". Although Ministers have ring-fenced a specific amount of money for adult and community learning (including family learning, learning for older people, active citizenship, community development learning and learning through cultural activities) the re-balancing between well-resourced parts of the country and poorly resourced areas is in danger of resulting in a levelling down rather than a levelling up.

LSC Essex has published its Statement of Priorities for 2005/6. I note, however, that while it includes vulnerable adult groups such as low skilled and unskilled workers, it does not include targets for the broader needs of communities (cultural, artistic, social and political). It may no longer be possible to fund the rich mix of learning that is currently provided in Colchester and elsewhere under the heading of "other further education". This would eliminate the very opportunities that prove attractive to new or returning adult learners.

The wording of the Learning and Skills Act means that the needs of 16-19 year olds must take priority. Adults get what is left. A rise in the size of the 16-19 cohort over the next five years, and the government's success in engaging more of them in education, will squeeze the public budget available for adults. The danger is that, just when economic and demographic trends call for increased support for adult learning, public sector cash will be less available than at any time since Labour came to power.

A further difficulty is that over the last ten years, funding has sometimes given incentives for education providers to stimulate demand through low fee (or even no-fee) offers to both individuals and employers. There are dangers lurking in the relentless pressure to be innovative (initiatives, projects, targets, audits) in return for project funding and to provide easy-to-measure outcomes in return for government attention. A more rational fees policy could open up increased funding, but such a change of direction will take time.

The Government wants to rationalise the way educational opportunities are provided, focusing on need rather than initiatives from particular providers. Reflecting this, LSC Essex wants to get employers more involved in planning the educational opportunities that are available and to ensure that there is strategically coordinated provider co-operation throughout the Essex area. Essex County Council, which is funded by LSC Essex and provides a very significant part of adult learning, is reviewing the way it organises its service through its existing adult community colleges. The position of governors in the new system is not yet decided, but it seems likely that there will be one governing body for the whole County service, with advisory committees in place locally.'

At the time of writing, an 'occupancy survey' of both Grey Friars and the Wilson Marriage Centre has been requested by County Hall. It is said that Essex County Council officials have been visiting local primary schools' playing fields, especially football pitches, tape measure in hand.

A study of the St Botolphs area master plan has revealed that some other Grade II listed property also owned by the County Council, is scheduled for disposal.

There is currently a battle raging in the press over the Borough Council's plans to close the bus station opposite Grey Friars. Local people are becoming very concerned about what may happen to the shape of their town as well as their much-loved historic architectural heritage.

12

Management

When you talk to tutors at Grey Friars they will tell you how easy it is to approach the senior management staff. This is an ethos started by the first principal and carried on by the present one. Although Allin was called Mr Coleman, Alan Skinner is simply known as Alan. And the senior staff are all called by their first names. Warmth and informality are the hallmarks of the college.

Senior Tutor for Languages

The newly appointed senior tutor for the language department has his office up on the top floor, where servants lived centuries ago. His attic room looks out over trees and roofs of Colchester.

Giovanni Gravina, a handsome, bearded Italian in his late thirties, was born in Sicily and came to the UK in 1996. At first, he was based in London, until marriage to an Ipswich girl and a job in Essex brought him to Colchester. Has he swapped Italy for England because of politics, money or romance?

He says, 'I wanted to change my life - that was why I came here. At first it was meant to be temporary. But I met my wife; she is English, so it is now money and love.' The two young children are bi-lingual. His six-year-old daughter can already speak both languages fluently.

Giovanni has always loved and studied languages. He speaks perfect English and Italian, can teach Spanish and studied French at university level. 'Through friends I met, I became a language tutor in Suffolk College.' He is very highly qualified. He has a degree and an MA in education and further qualifications in linguistics and the teaching of languages. Giovanni has taught in secondary schools and also in university. He finds teaching adults pleases him more. 'The students are so motivated that it is relaxing. They are very interesting people. They become not just my students, but some become friends.'

There appear to be no problems of behaviour in adult education. If there are, it is very rare. Giovanni likes the fact that in adult education students are not overloaded with course work as they may be at university. He appreciates the fact that his adult students are with him for the love of Italian language; they come from one year to the next. 'My language, my culture, and my history - adults appreciate them.'

Films are one of his specialities. He has organised a club which shows weekly, throughout the term, a first-rate foreign film. These films can also be borrowed by members for a nominal joining fee.

He is aware that government policies alter swiftly and that adult education does not attract the funding that secondary education does. 'I think that it is wrong because adult education is a fantastic invention.' He remarks that adult education as we have it in Colchester is unknown in Italy, except for a minority. 'Adult education here is a fantastic experience for *all* adults. It is not just about people coming to a class. You have people who are specialists in what they are doing, what they are learning. You get young people coming from sixth-form college or university. They enter the same class with adults and their experience of adult learning gives them the chance of being treated as adult so they present no behavioural problems - and no homework problems.'

Like many tutors, he could if he chose, apply for a university teaching position. He prefers to remain teaching adults. The Language department has around thirty-five tutors and offers 117 courses in languages including English as a foreign language. The main European languages such as French, German, Italian and Spanish are taught and there are also courses in languages like Russian, Arabic and Japanese.

In line with government policy, the courses tend towards accreditation. Of the 117 courses on offer, at least a fifth of them lead to some qualification ranging from the credit gained from completing an ASOCN (Anglia South Open College Network) course to GCSE and A Levels. The emphasis in the language department is now on accredited exam courses, 'Because these are the courses that get funding from the government.' Giovanni does not regret the examination ethos because he says it gives the students an aim and an attainable goal.

'I don't like being pushed into something, but exams are very good in that you have to pull everything together that you have been learning. It is a good way of measuring your abilities in that subject.' But he also appreciates the value of non-accredited courses. He says, 'We have to offer the community the possibility to study language whether they want an exam or not.'

Giovanni is proud that his students' pass rate is higher than the national average. 'The majority get very good results. Most of my GCSE students got grade A. The last exam they took was maybe twenty or thirty years ago so these are pretty good achievements.' I found it strange that French GCSE was not offered in 2004, but Giovanni says that it has been such a well-offered school subject that there was no call for it. 'The majority took it at school. In the future I will push into GCSE German and Russian. All our Russian A-level candidates passed at A grade.'

What would he change in the organisation of his college or department? 'As an institution I would provide more facilities. If you want to serve the community you have to offer more things like a lift and better IT facilities.' Giovanni is a moderniser. There has been a rumour that one day Grey Friars may be shut down and a custom-built educational facility be built in an outlying area of town. For some of us this would be a retrograde step. Utility taking precedence over tradition. Giovanni would not object to a new building. He says: 'I do like this building, but that would probably be a good thing in the long run. If you think of facilities it would be easier in a new building, bigger classrooms and better technical resources. It can be difficult to manage lessons in some of these old rooms. Lots of old windows, sash windows.'

Many of us would disagree with these ideas. Many would be sceptical about just how big and how well-equipped a replacement building may be. But without a doubt Giovanni is forging ahead to make the language department outstanding in its examination successes and the range of its courses.

Howard Leyshon

Howard is the longest-serving member of staff in the institution. It does not show. Short, pepper and salt beard, he is usually seen rushing somewhere. Like most Grey Friars staff, he doesn't go in for ostentation. He took us up to his little cubby-hole of an office on the top floor where it is said that a ghost of a monk walks, sat us down and talked of his early days.

'When I was 11, the headmaster came into woodwork and asked, "What's your aim in life, boys?" Derby, where I was brought up was mostly heavy industry, railways. "Fireman, engine driver," said most of the lads. He came to me and I said, "I want to be an art teacher." Really quite a weird response. I hadn't thought about it before. "I'd get a good pension," I told the headmaster. Quite astute for an 11 year old, I thought. When I was 16, I went to a local art college, moved on to Leicester College for my degree and Hornsey for an art teacher's certificate. I then ended up in Ulster for four years teaching kinetics to degree-level students. They wanted to bring that particular college into the 20th century. Not long before I had arrived the models were always draped.

In 1973 I came to Colchester as a tutor/organiser for Arts and Crafts. I was in Grey Friars - this very building - so I go back the longest. I was appointed by the original principal Allin Coleman, but as soon as I arrived he disappeared for a secondment so I carried on for two years with Ken Bushell, a temporary principal, very nice chap. Then Enid Bishop became principal and, on her retirement, Alan Skinner took the post – so I have worked for all the principals.'

Howard did a management diploma and, retaining an office in Grey Friars, became the LEA's county advisor for Arts and Crafts. 'Really most of my career, I have been here. I don't think originally I had much idea of what adult education meant. There was the hope there would be a great move forward under the Russell report in 1972, when Mrs Thatcher was Education Secretary. Russell felt that adult education was going to be the great new thing. The Report seemed very well received, but its promises unfortunately didn't materialise.'

Howard now has something of a missionary zeal in promoting learning for adults, although he wouldn't display this in an obtrusive manner. Like so many people involved with the teaching of adults, he simply loves it. 'There's an extra something in adult education that isn't there anywhere else. You're also learning in the company of friends really. I think that's a particularly nice thing that I treasure. People are moving forward, progressing – it's not just about learning but about people developing as people in the humanist sense and that is partly what inspired me.

Then there was a massive reorganisation and many posts disappeared. There was a change from a mixed service of adult, youth and community centres. The LEA formed the ten adult colleges in the county of which Grey Friars is one. They were set up with governors and principals, vice-principal for each one and so on. When that happened my County job disappeared and I had to go into the pot and apply for what was left. With the threat of redundancy, what better way to return to my roots than to go back to Colchester?'

Howard continues, 'I became the senior curriculum coordinator, then assistant principal.' Whatever the job, he has always had an office in the same building. Seniority bears no relation to size of office. And occupying the same tiny space for so long has given him he says, 'a genuine physical link between me and the building.'

Indeed, Howard has been involved with the development of the Grey Friars curriculum for over thirty years. 'Look at the collection of prospectuses. When I arrived it was less than one A4 size sheet folded down. One principal called the prospectus "handbag size".' Howard remarks how at first all the subjects were 'nice and comfortable' arts and crafts. There were only about four accredited subjects.

The number of courses offered rose gradually over the years. In 1966 there were 119 courses;1970 saw 309; by 1980 the number had risen to 542; in 1990 there were 995; and the choice peaked in 2000 with 1,020 courses on the curriculum.

'Particularly important to us now is choice and breadth of subjects and levels - providing the kind of courses that people in Colchester want. Many education authorities over the years have been strapped for cash so they have said no more adult education - that is why I am pleased Essex has kept it going. I think we have repaid them with great choice and high quality.'

That poorer students should pay little or no fees is essential, Howard says. 'Pensioners and the unemployed should provide proof of benefit that's all. Every course should be open. Just because a student is unemployed shouldn't mean they have to do a skill-based course. This is again something Essex ought to be proud of. There are nearly 50 thousand students in Adult Education across Essex of which we have got around ten thousand. We at Grey Friars are doing almost 20% of the county's work - a high figure for only one of ten colleges.

One of the strengths of Grey Friars and other similar institutions is the flexible nature of part time study. It appeals to all types of people. We can put on courses to test people's response, we can employ part time tutors, for quite short courses of varying lengths. This includes Summer School intensive courses and day-schools which I started in the art and crafts department and which have now spread across the curriculum. Summer School is one of the jewels in the Grey Friars crown. You only need to speak to someone who does a short course to find how stimulated and challenged with the prospect of new skills they feel.'

Howard is proud of the growth of Summer School. 'From the cautious start of a couple of art-based courses, the Summer School has grown to something like one hundred and fifty courses which cover virtually every area including Special Needs – some office subjects even have exams at the end of a Summer School. It brings new people in because we build in a link with the autumn term curriculum.'

Howard is aware that national pressure to produce courses leading to employment conflicts with a local public need for courses that may not. 'What the public wants from us is not necessarily what other people, especially the holders of the public purse strings, want from us. How we want to manage the courses is not necessarily how other authorities want us to manage them.'

Concerning the wider picture, Howard says, 'Adult Education has always been the Cinderella of the education service. We always seem to be at the end of the line when it comes to funding. Obviously the available funding has first to be put into areas of mandatory education. Adult Education is not mandatory, although LEAs have a duty to ensure that something happens, but have hitherto not really been held to account.

Now, all our funding comes from the Learning and Skills Council which obviously has to fund with strings attached - an agenda set by government.' Howard refers to the government slant on adult education which wants courses which lead to employment. 'Government,' says

Howard, 'cares about jobs so they are interested in the kind of course that leads to jobs, in developing people to live more economically productive lives. Although there is some safeguarded funding for non-academic, non-vocational learning, it is very much about the economy now.' Grey Friars has had to address these government priorities. Training people for jobs is specific and something Grey Friars can do very well. But non-accredited courses are another issue and Howard, as an art teacher, is constantly concerned about them.

'Up to now we have kept a very good balance. We have achieved our LSC targets yet still keep courses like the 10-week embroidery course or the 5-week literature. I desperately believe it is so important that people come into this building not necessarily thinking that they want a job or expect an exam at the end of their course. They come in, they want to improve themselves, they want to learn - maybe do a pottery class or maybe a creative writing class. Through that route people develop in all sorts of ways. It is a question of preserving that balance.

The county LEA is now being funded as a service; they get all the money. We in the colleges don't get anything directly. We have to match in with that county agenda. What we are trying to do is fulfil national and county targets whilst finding ways of keeping the more individual, locally-relevant agendas across the colleges. Communities are not all the same across the county.'

When asked for an example, Howard says, 'We could be forced to drop our craft courses because they do not lead to employment. Folksy ones don't lead to modern jobs. But if we did not run them, the participants couldn't have the enjoyment and cultural and intellectual fulfilment they clearly do. Older people wouldn't have this facility. If adult education stopped tomorrow some crafts would struggle to survive.' Referring to the 1994 Ofsted Inspectors' report he says, 'Inspectors were impressed with the quality of the work we have been doing. But we are in a different regime now and although last year's Adult Learning Inspectors were privately impressed with our college, they were inspecting the whole county service and couldn't comment on us officially. And the relationship with our communities did not feature at all.'

Howard follows Alan Skinner's lead. 'He has a concept that our student body is made up of fee-paying volunteers - in other words their participation is not just based on the sale of a product. They willingly take part, contribute to the costs and also contribute in other social, cultural and professional ways, to the whole experience.'

And the future? 'The funding situation is going to be challenging. Adult Education has always been on the margin, but we are still here. Ten years ago we might have disappeared when there was a reorganisation. We survived last time so why not again?'

Diana McLeod

Diana, the vice principal is a lively woman in her fifties, one of those people whose smile has an immediacy that makes you smile back.

Diana was born and bred in Essex. Her parents both worked; her mother as a clerical assistant. Her father was a teacher, gaining a post as headmaster only a short time before his early death. Money was tight, but

it was never in question whether she would go to university.

Like many women in further education, she gave up secondary school teaching to have the first of her two children, but returned to teach evening classes only three weeks after the birth of her daughter. She later had another break in service of three months, taking time out to have her son. Her husband is a secondary school teacher. Diana has been full-time at Grey Friars since 1989, having previously taken a new direction by building a career in adult education based around part-time teaching and management posts. She envisages spending the rest of her working life in the college. She loves the day-to-day challenges of working in a vibrant institution whose staff and students are a fascinating mix of ages and cultures. 'It's nothing,' she said, 'to come across a group in the coffee bar engaged in a vociferous discussion of something completely in a foreign language. At times it's like living in a multi-lingual society!'

The changes that may come as a result of government funding priorities may well affect the structure of adult education in Essex. Diana is sure that, 'Whatever happens, people will want to come to Grey Friars in the same way. We want to continue to offer what local people want. We have to find ways of funding a wide curriculum and if that means we have to put up fees we will, but we will still do all we can to make sure that the people who can not afford the fees are offered concessions.'

Accessing sufficient funding to support an institution like Grey Friars is a perennial problem. 'Many non-vocational courses offered at Grey Friars are looked on with less favour by the funding organisations. The wider adult curriculum, with its support of minority-interest subjects such as some of the traditional arts and crafts, is less likely to provide the statistics on young persons' achievement that presently dominate politicians' educational priorities.'

The thinking emanating from County Hall doesn't always coincide with what senior management want for the college. They feel that it should provide a far-reaching service to the whole community – including older people, who make up about 25% of the college's student population; and that it should tailor that service to meet the specific needs of all sections of the local community, using resources within the framework set by national and local government, but according to locally-identified priorities.

When we asked Diana why she thought senior managers were sometimes out of step with 'county hall' thinking, she cites the inspection of 2004. This was done as a whole county exercise, covering as one 'service' all ten colleges including Grey Friars - giving only one set of grades for the combined colleges.

Diana gives an example, 'Across the county there was a low grade for IT (information technology). This made our tutors downcast as it did not reflect the reality of our own IT courses. It would have been the same had our provision been poor and the rest of the county excellent. You can't get a clear picture of your own college's progress if you are inspected lumped with other institutions which may have different priorities and different problems. How can you follow it up?'

Diana says, 'I don't go for one size fits all.' She points out the diversity even within the county of Essex. 'Harlow, Basildon, Colchester, Saffron Walden have different demographics and different needs, but within those areas there are significant, very localised, social and economic characteristics which can so easily be ignored. A standardised approach wouldn't be addressing community education needs properly.'

Many tutors at Grey Friars feel almost overwhelmed by the increase of paperwork, the keeping of records on a class-by-class basis. The nationwide introduction of ILPs (individual learning plans) provokes almost universal criticism. On an ILP the tutor should make notes, in prescribed ways (and using prescribed language such as "learning goals") which are checked by inspectors and possibly auditors. They have to record, each session, the student's attendance, what they have learned and what they need to do. This is in addition to any subject-based preparation that the tutor would in any case have for their course. With several arms and several pairs of eyes (and a lot more paid time) available to the teacher it could be accomplished. Also it seems impertinent to keep files on the 'progress' of experienced members of society. One wonders how a fitness tutor would tell an elderly person that they would have to note that unfortunately they had made no discernable progress that day. Alan Skinner said, on hearing that the County Council had decided to close Wansfell College (its only residential college for adults) 'Every cloud has a silver lining. At least the principal won't have to ask Sir Patrick Moore to fill in his ILPs and submit himself for training for the City & Guilds adult education teaching qualification when he's signed up for his next series of lectures!'

When Diana herself was teaching adults in the 70s and 80s, she didn't write more than brief notes as an aide memoire to keep in her own records where each student had got up to and what they needed to work on. But all the lessons were prepared meticulously, every student was involved and individual and group needs were attended to. Tutors at that time had the professional freedom to tailor their approaches to the diverse needs of their students without having to reshape their record-keeping schemes to fit standardised processes.

'If there is one main difference in the new era, it is that it seems that there is less trust in the professionals to organise an efficient and high-quality service. This is a great shame, because there is plenty of evidence of adult education managers striving for the highest standards long before the present audit and control systems were introduced. When I first came here I was not at all surprised to hear that the principal was as likely to dismiss a tutor for poor classroom performance - including inadequate record keeping - or to expel a disruptive student, as he was to take a risk and nurture a proven craftsperson to make them into a good teacher.

Some years ago I read an obituary for former Educational Centres Association Honorary Secretary Ray Lamb who from 1942 to 1976 worked to make his east London centre a high-quality college for adults. Alan Skinner was so impressed by Ray's story that he edited his professional life story for the ECA.[1] Perhaps if the powers that be had taken adult education seriously enough in the past and appointed carefully, giving senior staff sufficient flexibility and resources, we may have achieved a set of high standards nationwide, instead of the mixed bag of services we currently have. There is no doubt that this inconsistency across the country has led to the more draconian controls we now face.'

She says, and it makes complete sense in the context of Grey Friars, 'In theory ILPs are more suited to a Sixth Form college or to parts of a Further Education institution where students attend every day and have a personal tutor - we see our students usually only once a week. We do not and cannot have that ongoing intimate knowledge. I don't think the concept of ILPs suits adult students. However, it's all part of the culture of record keeping and measuring to standardise approaches and attempt to quantify the unquantifiable; and if that's what we have to do to keep the funds coming in to deliver the goods to our students - so be it!'

Diana, ever an optimist, can see some advantage to tutors if the government does reduce funding for non-accredited courses. 'This *should* reduce paperwork automatically, as government may be less interested in precise, measurable outcomes for the money they give.'

She points out that at current prices (2004) the cost of delivering one hour's tuition is £80 – a sum which includes all the infrastructure and resources to ensure that a professionally managed service works within government funding guidelines. Clearly with an unpredictable number of students paying varying amounts of fees there is no guarantee that the actual cost of any course will be covered by the fees. Overall, fee payers contribute about 25% of their proportion of the real cost. Considering that many students in a class will be on a means-tested benefit and, therefore will not pay any tuition fee, the proportion of cost that students pay in any particular course will vary. ESOL and Skills for Life Literacy courses and similar activities are separately funded and free to all students. Fees will inevitably have to go up, she believes, but the service will have to continue to be supported by public funds.

Reference
1   Skinner, Alan ed. (2001)
        A Lifetime in the Education of Adults
        Contributions from Peter Baynes, Ronald Wilson, Peter Boshier,
        Harold Marks HMI, Bernard Godding, Brian Rainey, Brian Leighton,
        Peter Clyne, Prof Brian Groombridge and Prof Konrad Elsdon
        Educational Centres Association, Norwich www.e-c-a.ac.uk
        0870 161 0302

Alan Skinner – Principal of Grey Friars

Alan has been the principal at Grey Friars for over twenty-one years. He looks much as when I first met him in the early eighties. The smile is identical and his readiness to support his staff remains the same. Twenty-one years ago he had no idea that he would end up at Buckingham Palace with an MBE for his services to adult education.

About his early life, he says: 'Mother's family ran a newsagent's shop in Rotherhithe. During World War Two they experienced the horrific burning of Surrey Docks at first hand. Mum worked mostly for Marks & Spencers, but was very proud of her 'war work' in an engineering company. When I arrived in 1947 Dad insisted that Mum would not return to work - her job was to run the family, his was to provide.

Dad's was an army family living in Bermondsey. Grandfather was a Regimental Sergeant Major. If Dad had not married, he too may have become a career soldier. He was unlikely to have had a commission,

however, as he was happier being one of the troops. He was the eldest of four and went to work aged 14 to support the other three who all went to college. The boys went to university, their sister to secretarial college. All three gained good careers. Dad was a postman before WW2 and went back afterwards. He stayed with the GPO, latterly taking counter work. After retirement, he worked part-time as a clerk for the police. His early active life must have kept him fit as he was quite a successful road-race cyclist and enjoyed good health for most of his life before cancer finally defeated him in his eighties.'

For Alan's parents, education was the key to success. They encouraged and supported both boys to 'get educated'. He said , 'It must have worked better on my brother Robin (five years younger) who passed the 11+ and went to grammar school. I was unhappy at my primary school and reacted badly to the rigid, doctrinaire and sometimes brutal regime, although I was never bullied by fellow pupils. A combination of being physically bigger and quick-thinking kept me out of trouble with peers.

Most of my childhood memories are in monochrome – representative of the battered state of east London in the post-war years. My playgrounds were bomb sites and redundant air-raid shelters. The drab grey memories are relieved by two predominant colours – the shining scarlet of the London Transport buses and trolleybuses (always clean) and the bright green of the playing fields, reinstated after emergency use as allotments in wartime. We lived in 'rooms' in a multi-occupancy, dilapidated Victorian house until I was 15 when we were re-housed on a brand-new council estate. By then I had gained a place at Secondary Technical School, a halfway-house for 11+ failures who weren't fully relegated to the Secondary Modern system.

I enjoyed a good school career in social terms, getting involved in all kinds of activities, mostly based around music and writing, before becoming the first non-sporting-hero House Captain (although we still managed to win many sports trophies!) I learned a great deal during those years, although my academic achievements were unremarkable. I was originally in the Science and Engineering Division, failed all my GCEs, switched to Arts for the first year sixth and eventually passed both 'O's and 'A's - only just, though. The later school years were spent attempting to keep my places in the Hackney Schools' Orchestra, a local dance band and the estate cricket team. I also ran a little printing press and a buying-and-selling business from my room which gave me some financial independence - but not to the extent reached by Alan Sugar who was in my year at school. He did the same kind of thing, but went on to found Amstrad and other world-class businesses!'

Like Allin Coleman, Alan's predecessor at Grey Friars, Alan did not progress in an orderly way from secondary school to university.

'After leaving school in the 1960s I worked in a Sainsbury's store warehouse in Islington, for an office temp agency, the dance band put up with me and I worked most weekends. I set up a youth club with friends on our newly-finished housing estate and put on reviews in the community hall to large audiences (not all there in a supportive capacity!) - until Dad said "It's about time you set about getting a proper job, son" - meaning I should try to become a "professional".

At the Hackney Careers Service I was told that the only profession I was likely to suit was teaching. I applied to train as a teacher of English, first choice Goldsmith's, London, second choice Trent Park, Herts, which I finally attended in 1966. Goldsmiths' vice-principal tried to persuade me to take a place in the music department, referring to my grade C in A-level English: "Let's face it, you're not particularly brilliant at English." I didn't tell him I'd achieved that grade having only read half of the book list - the ones that interested me - and didn't answer all the exam questions!'

Government targets (yes, in the 1960s) intervened even at the start in my educational career as I was forced to undertake some primary-level training, although I had no intention of teaching the younger ones. We weren't allowed to train only for secondary level in English, there being an urgent need for primary teachers.

As at school, I learned as much through peripheral activities as through the syllabus. I was elected to the College Union and ran the publications department, responsible for the newspaper and literary journals, for three years. I got to know the principal well as a result of this, as controversy was the order of the day. "Not the kind of thing one would expect to see in publications from aspiring teachers" was the phrase most used by the principal when talking to me. Jack Straw headed the National Union of Students at that time and I made good use of their advice services. Needless to say, I wasn't invited back for a fourth-year conversion course to the new Bachelor of Education degree, despite a distinction in English (it was later, as a mature student, that I was to discover the enjoyable rigour of academic study) and set forth with my Certificate in Education to teach in a comprehensive school in Basildon.'

What he did learn very quickly, however, was how to use his wider experience outside the world of education to become a more effective teacher. 'I started at the same time as some others who had followed the traditional path: grammar school to college and back to school as a teacher. I didn't match this pattern, but far from regretting it, I was grateful for being able to relate not only to the students' social situations, but also relate subjects to my wider working experience. Watching some colleagues struggle to engage with their classes I became convinced that anyone entering the teaching profession should have a compulsory period working in another environment before taking a post, plus occasional placements thereafter. I am sure that is why so many adult education teachers can bring so much more to their students.'

Initially, he started to teach adults less as a mission, more as a way of augmenting a low salary. 'As new teachers, we were allowed to rent a council flat. I discovered that I could apply for a rent rebate as my wages were significantly lower than the norm at the time and 14/6d was rebated from the weekly rent of two pounds, fourteen shillings and sixpence. It was still a struggle so when my colleague Paddy suggested that I take over his evening class as he wanted to spend more time with his young family, I telephoned the Evening Institute and asked how to apply. The answer came "Don't worry about that, Paddy has told me all about you - you can take over next term".

I duly arrived at a neighbouring school to teach "English for Office Workers" and found them more apprehensive of me than any school pupil had been, sitting towards the back of the classroom, hiding behind the chairs which had been put on top of the desks at the end of the school day. I learned as much as they did that term. I learned about adult learners' motivations, fears, previous poor experiences of education, previous lost or wasted opportunities, sacrifices in order to return to learning. I learned that there were as many reasons for being there as there were people in the room. I learned to be less judgemental about peoples' lives; to think carefully about how I operated in my schoolteacher role; and to be less annoyed when I found "night school" cigarette butts in the inkwells in my own classroom. This early experience also opened my eyes to the potential of adult education – and, sadly, to the parlous state of its funding, organisation and management, position on the periphery of the world of education and, worst of all, low esteem in the eyes of the general population.'

After two years in Basildon he moved to a promotion in South Ockendon, then to Head of the English Department in Tilbury. This was concurrent with part-time evening class work, latterly as a head of centre. At that stage, with a new degree and successful track record, a move to a larger management role beckoned. Did he regret the idea of leaving the classroom for a desk job?

'I didn't see it that way. As far as I was concerned, management was as much about activity and practical work, participation if you like, as it was about administration. Therefore, I would approach any managerial role through active leadership, dealing with strategy of course, ensuring efficient administration of course - but leading from the front. I'd seen too many instances of remote management, often by people who thought being the boss meant you had to be 'bossy' and didn't need to get your hands dirty any more, to make that mistake myself and as a result ruin the potential of colleagues and our pupils by not sharing responsibility, delegating and developing a team.'

There then followed a period of enquiries, applications and interviews in schools, FE and adult education. His 'leading from the front' and practical approach cost him the post of deputy headmaster in one school for being just that - 'The chairman of governors said that I came across as what I now see as too much of the 1980s equivalent of the modern 'team player' - he said I would not be remote enough for such a position - how times change!' He declined a job offered at the Technical College as his timetable would comprise compulsory English with very reluctant teenage plumbers, bricklayers and hairdressers. He had an unsuccessful interview for the post of deputy headmaster at the biggest comprehensive in Kent (after interminable delays it went to the internal candidate). Then he was offered the post of principal at Grays Adult Centre. Joining the world of adult learning meant an immediate and substantial pay cut.

'I upset the County official who appointed me by asking if I could bring my salary up to what I was earning in school by getting paid for teaching evening classes over my hours at the Centre. It was pointed out that there was no such thing as 'over my hours' as I was on a full-time contract and all of my time at the Centre belonged to the County Council. I had never counted hours up until then, but was tempted to start doing so, but the fervour of colleagues, the enthusiasm of the students and the potential for development soon motivated me and I set out to build up the professional and academic profile of local adult learning.

I had been spurred on to try to help adult education gain a better position in the education world by the headmaster's speech on my leaving day. He said he couldn't understand why I was leaving a promising career to go to teach adults to read and organise keep fit for ladies. Although this may only have been a joke alluding to the advantages of leaving the school environment, it was too near to the conventional wisdom on adult learning to be ignored. It constituted a challenge. I was also visited by a County inspector just after I resigned and he said that he wanted to be sure that I was aware of what I was going into before I turned my back on a promising career in schools. He was obviously alluding to the poor pay, resources and low status in adult education.'

Rising to what he saw as a challenge, Alan set about some practical tasks to raise the profile of local adult education.

'Therefore, the first thing I did in my new job was to remove the small 'Grays Adult Centre' sign and raid the LEA's store for old desk lids which the caretaker and I cut out into letters. The carefully shaped and painted large new letters spelt out 'Grays Adult *Education* Centre'. We then successfully launched a series of new exam classes specially designed for adults – much to the annoyance of senior staff at the local FE college who told me that they depended on adults to make viable their classes for youngsters - and then made some very derogatory remarks about the nature of part-time tutors. I was henceforward known locally as 'the man who put the education into Grays Adult Centre'! I then wanted to go further and raise the professional profile of the whole adult education sector, locally and nationally.'

He made applications and was invited for interview to two posts on the same day. One was in Kent and the other Essex. 'In those days, interviews were generally about 45 minutes and sudden death – you either got the job then and there, or were rejected. Both interviews were in the morning. I called the Kent office to ask if there was the possibility of me attending both by juggling times to either end of the day, but the chief inspector said that if I wasn't serious about their job I shouldn't bother. I was serious, but his attitude had made the decision for me. I turned up at County Hall, Chelmsford, was fortunate in seeing the previous candidate (who seemed my closest rival) come out in a fury at something that had been said and was duly appointed to be the principal at Colchester in November 1983.'

During his time at Grey Friars much has happened to adult education nationally and locally. Alan had to re-apply for his post when Essex County Council reorganised adult education in 1992, amalgamating the separate centres into colleges serving wider areas. 'It was very strange arriving at County Hall for interview and being sincerely wished the very best of luck by two of my nine rivals for the post of principal at Colchester.'

He was re-appointed, however, as was the vice-principal Diana McLeod and they were joined by Howard Leyshon, who had previously been offered another post, but turned it down to return to Grey Friars.

There then followed a period of great change in the post-school sector, but Grey Friars (with its new title The Adult Community College, Colchester) continued to thrive educationally and organisationally. Grey Friars staff, Members' Association officials and governors were active in promoting adult education locally and nationally, giving seminars and lectures to fellow professionals, and responding to government consultations on the development of the post-school education sector. Alan is adamant that this involvement was professionally, not personally, motivated. 'We spoke from experience, from the heart and with genuine concern about adult learning opportunities. At that time there was not a hint of any personal agendas or empire-building. We were received as expert and dedicated participants.'

The report of Ofsted's 1995 inspection gave colleagues confidence:

Students are well catered for and overall standards of achievement across the college are good. In 30% of the classes achievement was satisfactory; in 55% good and in 15% very good.

Students are confident, serious learners and make good progress. In some areas of the curriculum, such as art and craft, students achieve high standards and produce excellent work.

Students participate fully in the classes and learn with enthusiasm; they support each other and benefit from well organised and carefully planned sessions.

The quality of learning was satisfactory in 21% of classes; good in 66% and very good in 13%.

Teaching staff ensure work is challenging and demanding, are skilled, know their subject well and communicate effectively with students. 97% teaching is satisfactory or better; 76% was good or very good.

Staff support students in a positive manner and encourage them to extend themselves.

The college has a committed and loyal student body.

Enrolment rates are high and retention rates generally good.

This is a cost-effective service, but there are some limitations in the low full-time staffing level.

Ofsted wanted to inspect the Essex Adult Education Service as it was at the time, but County officials told them that the service was too big and complicated, so HMI decided to visit Colchester and use it as an indicator of the County service. How ironic this is in the light of recent developments where, as Essex claimed responsibility for funding and quality, there had to be one inspection covering all colleges as if they were a combined unit.

The 1995 report was the best for an LEA adult college for at least three years and on behalf of the students and tutors, it was very satisfying, but management colleagues were concerned with some of the other comments. Alan gives an example.

'The detail of the report gave some clear warnings about the future of adult education. We were aware that all the time we were being judged against the better-funded FE colleges. And our status as an off-shoot of County Hall would give us problems in responding to the recommendations, especially where overall strategies and resources were concerned. The inspectors said that the budget was "efficiently monitored but not strategically managed". As far as we were concerned we were able to do the former, but the latter was not fully within our powers. They also made some comments about curriculum with which we didn't necessarily agree, obviously assuming that we had more local autonomy than was really the case.

Nevertheless, we gradually built up management systems to reflect the FE sector, as well as extending the breadth of our curriculum. How tragic now, after nearly ten years of struggling to reach those standards, to find that the goalposts are about to be moved and we are now no longer expected to behave as a college, but must take our managerial lead from County Hall to an extent never before experienced. The fact that there had been a single inspection of ten colleges as if they were one unit made that quite clear - and in the process rendered our previous efforts almost irrelevant. The only solace we could take was that key members of our staff, such as Lindsay Baxter, our Quality and Development expert, were able to provide valuable assistance on a County level whilst others kept going locally. Nevertheless, we will continue to present what is essentially a national and local government-driven service in a way which makes it as relevant as possible to the local community.'

Does not a commitment such as this interfere too much in the life of a family man? 'Of course that is an issue, but I have always believed it is up to the individual to prevent it getting out of hand' he explains. 'I apply certain rules. I never take any work home and I do not expect to take work-related telephone calls at home except in emergency situations. That at least keeps a separation between home life and work life. Ok I do put in a lot of time at work, but when I'm not at work other priorities come into force.'

What does concern Alan is the increased pressure put upon managers and senior staff, 'Not just for me, but for colleagues and friends, I feel that whereas we have always worked hard and we possibly chose to put in too many hours in the past, it now seems necessary to do even more. But the essential difference seems to be that *we* used to be able to prioritise our efforts, balance it all out and gain a sense of achievement - even fulfilment.'

Alan takes a particular perspective on the increase of directives from government (national and local) and the increase in bureaucracy and intervention. 'Too often now, we run to stand still - and increasingly within an environment where we are not sure what we have achieved because the direction has either been conceived elsewhere and not communicated very well, or we are running on shifting sands. It is not good to go home to the family feeling tired *and* unfulfilled. Those who set the parameters for public services like education, social services and health need to be more aware of the effect of working practices on their staff. Too often at present these matters are addressed merely in glib phrases. Despite being dressed in the political correctness of "policies for health and safety, equal opportunities and work-life balance", as there is now so much to be done to reach targets and address quality criteria, the modern working life of an education professional has the potential to damage their families.'

In the late 1990s Alan was elected to the post of vice chairman of the Educational Centres Association (a charitable organisation of 80 years' national and international standing working to promote awareness and active participation by all concerned in adult learning).

He also chaired the Board of the Colchester Learning Shop through its first three years as a limited company and registered charity. It gives impartial educational information advice and guidance to local people. 'The Learning Shop (described in chapter 10) exemplified the first-ever real partnership between all the major post-16 educational providers in the Borough. The University of Essex, Colchester Institute, Sixth Form College, Anglia Polytechnic University, The Open University and Grey Friars were joined by the Borough Council in a unique partnership to fund a totally independent advice service for adults.

'As a representative forum able to use the feedback from its users to stay in touch with people's needs, the potential for such a partnership to break down barriers to access to learning – including cutting down on wasteful over-provision or competition – is so great, I would like it to continue to grow in order to fully co-ordinate the area's post-16 curriculum. This can be done without threatening any institution's own status or viability. It is achievable by the people concerned, but I have severe reservations as to whether it will ever reach its potential unless the government of the day and its quangos get to grips with funding arrangements, bureaucracy and the audit culture. Over the last ten years I have seen too many excellent policies from ministers reduced to a series of short-term statistic-massaging ploys, rather than providing tangible and sustainable improvements to local learning opportunities. Local managers in post-16 education institutions are fully capable of collaborating for the benefit of their communities – provided they are given back some of the local autonomy they have lost over the years.' But would not regaining autonomy lead them to revert to some of the un-coordinated and competitive practices of the past? Not necessarily, Alan says.

'Provided the truly beneficial changes of past decades can be maintained (such as more accessibility to learning for non-traditional adult participants, greater strategic awareness, clearer analysis of outcomes, less empire-building and more collaborative planning) managers should be able to be trusted as knowledgeable professionals, liberated from some of the more wasteful bureaucratic shackles. It would be far better if they were made more accountable to their local communities than to corporate bodies based at desks - scores, sometimes hundreds, of miles away.

There is still the possibility of much more funding supplying local needs if effective arrangements are made to charge local managers with the more relevant financial, organisational and educational responsibilities. The cohorts of administrators would be far better working to satisfy local needs than providing never-ending streams of data to bodies which are largely unproductive in enabling practical development of people's education and skills, but very effective in diverting resources from the front line. Also, the education service can work more effectively without significant numbers of people travelling around to sit in interminable meetings, talking rather than doing.'

His fascinating file entitled *Irritating Bureaucracy* contains evidence of 'instances where other people spend money from already top-sliced budgets supposedly delegated to us for teaching and learning - and then hold us to account for overspending; unbelievable multi-layering of managerial responsibility together with checking-up-on-people, draining funds which should get to the sharp end; ridiculous rules and regulations about corporate identity and outrageous sums spent on it; examples of the mangling of the English language in official documents - desperately near to George Orwell's 1984 newspeak; piles and piles of nonsense turning me prematurely into a Grumpy Old Man.'

He gestures around his office - to the bookcases full of files and especially to piles of expensive-looking colourful documents. There are government papers, policy briefings, consultations, analyses of responses to consultations, government and county council guidance documents, funding guides, quality manuals, and statistical analyses.

'Try and keep this lot tidy' he says with a rueful grin. 'Because they're so glossy they're slippery. Doesn't that just say it all!'

'The curriculum that has developed at this college over 60 years is not the result of an ad hoc collection of goodies to entertain the already-educated. To suggest so, and I have heard this many times, is to insult the professional contribution of every Grey Friars principal since the college began. Each has made their mark on the development of what has become regarded as a significant educational presence in the Borough. I must pay tribute to my predecessors. Allin Coleman built it up from the beginning, established its presence and set the tone for the people-orientated college it has become. Ken Bushell, here for a short time on secondment, consolidated the welcoming ethos. Enid Bishop widened the curriculum to set the tone for the high academic achievement of the 1980s and established the college as a springboard for higher education for adults. I therefore inherited a curriculum which has become the hallmark of the service – a wide-ranging, multi-entry-point, non-hierarchical range of learning opportunities for local people to enjoy.'

But isn't there a conflict between aiming to provide an educational experience that may be informal, relaxed and enjoyable, and wanting to taken seriously as a part of the educational 'mainstream'?

'That really shouldn't be an issue. If people enjoy the experience they will be relaxed and learn more easily. Enabling people to enjoy their learning is not a crime against the profession – it is good practice. If the tutors are professional in their preparation, organisation and keep up with their subjects then the standards of achievement will be high. We didn't get all those top national awards (chapter 9) by accident. High standards speak for themselves and awareness of people's achievements can negate criticism from uninformed commentators.

What we must protect, however, is the breadth of the curriculum. The only kind of curriculum relevant to adults' complicated lives is a comprehensive curriculum. This college is dedicated to the provision of a comprehensive curriculum for our local community. In such a curriculum no subject and no level is held to be more important than another, there is no hierarchy of motivation for learning and we are dedicated to supporting the widest range of learning opportunities for all adults. Although we always strive for the highest standards, we provide something more substantial than an educational ladder – our curriculum is more like a series of climbing frames - for our students, 'progression' can be made in all directions. We are as happy to see our learners widen their experience as we are for them to reach the highest levels. That is the true nature of a relevant adult education service.'

Alan told me his story over several meetings. Will he see a return to more local community relevance for adult education, or will the bureaucracies tighten their grip?

In the well-established, tried and tested Grey Friars tradition, he is committed to 'lifelong learning for all' and 'the development of a culture of learning throughout society' - phrases reassuringly repeated by government agencies over the last decade. But how will the funding cake be shared out between services for those students working for qualifications and those who are learning for less tangible results? It must be an equitable division because a service which is so valuable to communities as well as individuals should continue to be a public service, publicly funded.

[DS]

All four Grey Friars principals
Left to right: Allin Coleman (1960s-70s), Ken Bushell (seconded from Braintree College 1973), the late Enid Bishop (1970s-80s), Alan Skinner (1983-2005).

Postscript

Those involved with a flourishing, successful well-run institution never imagine that it will change – except, it is to be hoped, for the better.

Rumours in the local press about Essex County Council planning to sell Grey Friars were met with scepticism. However, in May 2005 there were some developments. A report, dated before the elections, but not made public until afterwards, was passed to the governors. It stated that the scheme to install a lift at Grey Friars was to be withdrawn because 'the cost was too great for a building which is listed for potential sale'.

The Members' Association, led by student governor Peter Marsh, called an Open Forum at Grey Friars on June 16th 2005. Its aim was to help with communications and clarify the complicated situation surrounding adult education in general and Grey Friars in particular. More than seventy people turned up, filling the Grey Friars hall.

The Forum was told that Grey Friars was indeed 'on a list of properties for review', but it was not (yet) subject to firm plans for disposal and the way was still open for local people to exercise their democratic rights and voice their opinions on the proposal.

However, the idea that Grey Friars could indeed become a block of luxury flats or a hotel created a feeling of gloom and despair in the audience. Many of those present remembered the mid-1980s, when a similar proposal was overturned by public opinion. However, although the shock and anger were the same, this time there didn't seem to be the same confidence that the sale could be stopped. But determination was in the air and the meeting mandated the chairman to begin a protest campaign, prime targets being local county councillors and the County Council's corporate decision-makers.

There were other pressing issues. A speculative suggestion that Grey Friars could be sold was bad enough. Now, in addition, there were rumours about funding cuts and the loss of college status. These issues heralded a new direction for the funding and organisation of adult education – all of which had direct bearing on what was to happen to Grey Friars, both its building and its identity.

Students wanted to know why there were cuts, who was making them and how they affected Grey Friars. The principal's reply quoted the official Learning and Skills Council announcement on its funding priorities which states that nationally they aim to make learning 'demand-led', to ensure that all 14-19 year olds have access to high quality, relevant learning opportunities, and to 'transform FE so that it attracts and stimulates business investment'.

Furthermore, locally, LSC Essex aims to 'increase the numbers of adults participating on their first full level 2 programme (equivalent of 5 GCSEs grades A-C) and targeted level 3 (A-level equivalent) provision'. They also intend to 'meet priority skills needs and prioritise basic skills training that leads to a qualification'.

Alarmingly, the only specific mention of wider, non-vocational adult education came in the national LSC document 'Reforming the funding and planning arrangements for First Step and Personal and Community Learning for Adults'. It proposed radical changes, but its implementation has been delayed for almost a year. This hiatus has unsettled the planning arrangements of many local authorities and kick-started reviews in anticipation of the effects of the new system.

Funding cuts are, in any case, likely to be deep and widespread. Essex LSC has already warned the County that there is to be a reduction of around 10% in the funding for 'adult further education' (exam and vocational courses, including the national priorities). It is clear that nationally the LSC is giving priority to younger people. In Essex that is likely to mean a greater reduction in adult education funding in order to cope with the higher success rates in the education and training of all age groups.

The discontinuation of payments for recruitment and retention of students beyond the targets set by the LSC has already resulted in a steep drop in income for Grey Friars (as discussed in chapter 11). The latest prospect of reductions in LSC contributions makes this worse – but there is a further problem: other opportunities to top-up Grey Friars' finances are receding as a consequence of the LEA's centralisation of bidding and funding arrangements which prevent colleges from operating freely within their own areas. Adult education in Essex is now financed as one service.

The college is 'over-achieving' its allocated targets. Bringing people into learning in ever-increasing numbers was once lauded as success, but in the present climate it is being defined as poor management. The college has over-reached itself in terms of its place in the new system - and has to cut back.

The college once operated according to the principle that it was possible to operate in a business-like manner, whilst avoiding treating education as a business. It seems that the contract culture now prevalent in the funding of public services, together with the new corporate approach of the local authority, have put an end to this notion.

Adult education must address changing national priorities, whether or not these are shared by the local people for whom the services are provided. This is especially the case for Grey Friars as yet another County Council reorganisation gets under way.

It is becoming apparent to students and staff that local managers' grip on the affairs of the college – so necessary to maintain cohesiveness in a complicated environment – is becoming weaker at the same time as external influences are becoming more powerful.

Government and funding bodies have historically been seen as 'outside' influences, but now it transpires that Essex County Council, once a protective hand in times of threat, is in fact exacerbating the problem through pursuit of corporate identity and control, including the desire to turn assets such as Grey Friars into cash. This is rapidly eroding the previously appreciated local identity and relevance of the County's adult education service.

In 1995 HMIs from Ofsted gave Grey Friars the highest gradings for quality of teaching and learning the sector had seen for years (chapter 12). As for the results of last year's (2004) Adult Learning Inspectorate (ALI) inspection there was no way of telling how Grey Friars had performed. According to an ALI official the college may exist as an identifiable unit in the eyes of local people, but to the ALI it is only one part of the Essex County Council Adult Education Service.

A similar situation now applies to funding contracts. It was once possible to go to the LSC offices to negotiate for funding. A hard bargain could be driven, quoting Colchester-relevant factors. It was also possible to supplement basic funding with additional contracts if they could be accommodated within the college's resources. Thus, Grey Friars could determine curriculum direction and be sure of funding the following year's activity.

At inauguration ten years ago, each college developed its own way of operating – a responsibility placed upon the principals in the 1994 reorganisation. But, in preparation for the 2004 ALI inspection, County sought to exert a swift and unprecedented level of central control. The result was a costly and frustrating duplication of management and planning activities. In pursuit of a county-wide identity, those systems already operating in each college were overlaid by the County's new arrangements. Inevitably, this could not continue and a review ensued, followed by reorganisation. The nine colleges are now being restructured into four area organisations with overall strategic direction determined on a county-wide basis.

As the autumn term 2005 nears its end, the combined effects of financial difficulties and reorganisation begin to take effect. Grey Friars, however, carries on - albeit with a reduced programme and fewer teachers and managers. One significant casualty is the swimming programme, a model of excellence in curriculum design (see chapter 7) where all courses have been withdrawn except for teacher training. Tutors and managers have been made redundant or have left. The principal has accepted redundancy and taken early retirement. The 'Skills for Life' manager and the vice principal have been transferred to other areas.

Grey Friars has developed as a living, breathing, working institution over its thirty or more years. It has changed with the times, adjusted its approach, but always managed to adapt in order to stay faithful to the core values of interactive and inclusive community education.

These are the same values enunciated by early principals such as Allin Coleman and reiterated by Alan Skinner. Whether you study painting, cake decorating, maths A Level, basic English or Italian for your holiday, you come to Grey Friars to learn. Whatever your age and motivation you are welcome. Now it seems that this inspirational college that has meant so much to so many people is under threat.

Grey Friars has served the people of Colchester well - now may be the time for those same people to mobilise and save it. The Members' Association public meeting of June 2005 and the subsequent lobbying of county councillors indicate that this process has begun.

Acknowledgements

The Educational Centres Association (ECA) provided funds to pay for the writing of this book and a legacy from E. Joan Gray paid for the production and printing costs.

The writers wish to acknowledge the help and support of the people whose stories appear in this book. The willingness of the interviewees to allow their stories to appear for the interest and inspiration of others is one of the book's most valuable aspects.

Grateful thanks go to the enormous number of people who have made a contribution - time, advice, practical help, information or financial donation, often anonymous - to the production of this book. Amongst them are B.A.B. Barton, Margaret Bearman, Pat Brown, Mary Brunning, Jill Butcher, John Cooper-Hammond, Ted Crunden, Mrs B.I.Dartnall, Sarah Denney, Dr Ian G.Dewis, Annie Fair, Alan Farncombe, Miss J.Fensome, Janet Fulford, Mrs Sheila Gordon, G. Gravina, Joan Gurney, Ms Margaret Handley, Dr Jane Heath, Iris Jones, Jenny Jones, Mrs M. Knight, Jane Lawrance, Josette Lord, Mrs P. Maltby, Diana McLeod, Linda Michael, Roger Moores, Claire Nixon, Sheena Parks, Brenda Pey, Jim Pey, Andrew Phillips, Mrs Shirley Ratcliffe, Susan Robbins, Mrs C.J. Roberts, Bob Russell MP, Sheila Scott, Alan Smith, Sylvia Skinner, Margaret R.Tarr, Patricia Tomson, I. L Thurston, Mrs S Tye, William Tyler, Julie Walters and Christine Wakeling.

The Members' Association will be placing inscribed copies of the book in the Grey Friars library in memory of Derek Lamberth, a dedicated and supportive chairman of the Advisory Committee (the precursor of the Board of Governors) and Geoffrey Underwood, an excellent, hard-working and utterly dedicated registrar.

Othet inscribed copies will mark the Association's appreciation of Reg Kearns, a long serving, flexible, dedicated and reliable caretaker, of John Thompson, the wholly supportive Area Community Education Officer who enabled Grey Friars to grow and prosper under Essex County Council in the 1980s and of Senior Tutors and Tutors, valued colleagues, too numerous to mention individually, who have contributed so much to the development of the college and enthused their students over the decades.